The Complete Guide to
Using Candlestick Charting:

How to Earn High Rates of Return — Safely

By Alan Northcott

The Complete Guide to Using Candlestick Charting: How to Earn High Rates of Return – Safely

Copyright © 2009 Atlantic Publishing Group, Inc.
1405 SW 6th Avenue • Ocala, Florida 34471 • Phone 800-814-1132 • Fax 352-622-1875
Web site: www.atlantic-pub.com • E-mail: sales@atlantic-pub.com
SAN Number: 268-1250

ISBN-13: 978-1-60138-294-8   ISBN-10: 1-60138-294-4

Northcott, Alan, 1951-
   The complete guide to using candlestick charting : how to earn high rates of return-safely / by Alan Northcott.
      p. cm.
   Includes bibliographical references and index.
   ISBN-13: 978-1-60138-294-8 (alk. paper)
   ISBN-10: 1-60138-294-4 (alk. paper)
   1. Stocks--Charts, diagrams, etc. 2. Stock price forecasting. 3. Investment analysis. I. Title.

   HG4638.N67 2009
   332.63'2042--dc22
                        2009007561

INTERIOR LAYOUT DESIGN: Nicole Deck • ndeck@atlantic-pub.com
BACK COVER DESIGN: Holly Gibbs • hgibbs@atlantic-pub.com

Printed on Recycled Paper

Printed in the United States

We recently lost our beloved pet "Bear," who was not only our best and dearest friend but also the "Vice President of Sunshine" here at Atlantic Publishing. He did not receive a salary but worked tirelessly 24 hours a day to please his parents. Bear was a rescue dog that turned around and showered myself, my wife Sherri, his grandparents Jean, Bob and Nancy and every person and animal he met (maybe not rabbits) with friendship and love. He made a lot of people smile every day.

We wanted you to know that a portion of the profits of this book will be donated to The Humane Society of the United States. –*Douglas & Sherri Brown*

The human-animal bond is as old as human history. We cherish our animal companions for their unconditional affection and acceptance. We feel a thrill when we glimpse wild creatures in their natural habitat or in our own backyard.

Unfortunately, the human-animal bond has at times been weakened. Humans have exploited some animal species to the point of extinction.

The Humane Society of the United States makes a difference in the lives of animals here at home and worldwide. The HSUS is dedicated to creating a world where our relationship with animals is guided by compassion. We seek a truly humane society in which animals are respected for their intrinsic value, and where the human-animal bond is strong.

Want to help animals? We have plenty of suggestions. Adopt a pet from a local shelter, join The Humane Society and be a part of our work to help companion animals and wildlife. You will be funding our educational, legislative, investigative and outreach projects in the U.S. and across the globe.

Or perhaps you'd like to make a memorial donation in honor of a pet, friend or relative? You can through our Kindred Spirits program. And if you'd like to contribute in a more structured way, our Planned Giving Office has suggestions about estate planning, annuities, and even gifts of stock that avoid capital gains taxes.

Maybe you have land that you would like to preserve as a lasting habitat for wildlife. Our Wildlife Land Trust can help you. Perhaps the land you want to share is a backyard— that's enough. Our Urban Wildlife Sanctuary Program will show you how to create a habitat for your wild neighbors.

So you see, it's easy to help animals. And The HSUS is here to help.

THE HUMANE SOCIETY
OF THE UNITED STATES.

2100 L Street NW • Washington, DC 20037 • 202-452-1100
www.hsus.org

Table of Contents

Table of Contents   **4**

Foreword   **9**

Preface   **11**

Chapter 1: The History of Candlestick Charting   **15**

Chapter 2: Introduction to Candlestick Charting   **25**

Chapter 3: Basic Construction of the Candle Line   **31**

Chapter 4: Basic Trading Strategies   **39**

Chapter 5: The Psychology of the Candles   **43**

The Doji 44

The Spinning Top 46

High Wave Candle 47

The Long Body 48

Chapter 6: Candlestick Patterns — Single-Day Reversal Signals   51

Chapter 7: Candlestick Patterns — Two-Day Reversal Signals   65

Chapter 8: Candlestick Patterns — Three-Day Reversal Signals   93

Chapter 9: Candlestick Patterns — Four-Day Reversal Signals and Beyond   129

Chapter 10: Candlestick Patterns — Two-Day Continuation Signals   145

Chapter 11: Candlestick Patterns — Three-Day Continuation Signals   155

Chapter 12: Candlestick Patterns — Four-Day Continuation Signals and Beyond   165

Chapter 13: Application of Candlestick Charting   173

The Place for Candlesticks 174

The Limitations of Candlesticks 174

The Advantages of Candlesticks 175

Blended Candle 176

Patterns to Watch 178

Chapter 14: Candlestick Confirmations   183

Moving Averages 184

Oscillators 185

Support and Resistance 197

Trendlines 199

Bollinger Bands 201

Volatility 202

Fibonacci 203

The Trading Plan 209

Chapter 15: Trading Psychology   209

Fear and Greed 212

Other Emotions 215

Trading Journal 216

Placing Your Trade 219

Chapter 16: Money Management   219

Trading Funds 223

Approach to Allocation 224

Making Your Picks 226

Figuring Your Stops 228

Sakata's Method 233

Chapter 17: Other Charting Methods   233

Three-Line Break 240

Renko Charts 245

Kagi Charts 248

Candle Volume Charts 253

Appendix A: Practice Charts   261

Chart of Lumber Liquidators, Inc. 262

Chart of Companhia Parana De Energ 266

Books 269

Appendix B: Resources   269

Web sites 271

Appendix C: Glossary   273

Author Dedication & Biography   283

Index   285

Foreword

Alan Northcott's *The Complete Guide to Using Candlestick Charting*, is an excellent resource for those interested in using Japanese candlestick analysis profitably. His depth in analyzing the extensive library of candlestick signals, along with their psychological implications, is truly commendable.

Northcott guides the reader through all the possible signals in a fast-paced, yet detailed manner. He then uses his research to get the readers to focus on those few "high probability" candlestick signals, which can provide plenty of trading opportunities daily. I would also like to highlight Northcott's effort in focusing on money-management techniques. Many books are written with emphasis only on reading charts and utilizing technical analysis. They miss out on this key issue, which incorporates correct use of stop-losses. Any trader can take a profit. It is only those traders who can control their losses that come out winners in the long run.

Trading has much to do with the psychology of the traders participating in the market. It is all about taking advantage of the fear and greed of other traders, while controlling your own. This makes it imperative to understand the emotional dynamics behind the entity one is trading. Candlesticks provide the most effective charting system to analyze this investor sentiment. The visual display of bearish and bullish sentiment provides the trader with a time-proven, easy-to-use analytical tool. Northcott has done an excellent job in conveying this message to the readers.

Plenty of traders jump in the market without a clue as to why stock prices move the way they do. The most common impression is that the fundamentals of a company move the stock price. This might hold true a few days of the trading year. However, the majority of the time, stock prices move because of a **change in the perception** of those fundamentals. This change of perception is depicted visually in the form of a candlestick. Correct interpretation of these candlestick signals can lead traders to extreme profitability.

However, as Northcott mentions in the book, it is important to use candlesticks with other technical indicators to confirm the validity of the signal. As research has shown, candlesticks cannot be used as a standalone system. Using a combination of candlestick signals and technical analysis creates a high probability trading scenario. It is highly recommended for any trader to indulge only in these trades which offer higher odds of success.

As the founder of Profitable Candlestick Charting and an experienced candlestick trader, I am proud to recommend this book to beginner and advanced traders alike. This book is packed with some serious money-making ideas. Along with its emphasis on capital preservation and risk assessment, the book presents fresh insights into new trading strategies. All in all, *The Complete Guide to Using Candlestick Charting* is a must own for any serious technical trader who wishes to successfully and profitably navigate the stock market.

Good luck and happy trading.

Balkrishna Sadekar

Founder, Profitable Candlestick Charting, LLC

www.ProfitableCandlestickCharting.com

Preface

If you have ever desired to take part in the ever-changing world of trading on the stock market, one of the most important things for you to learn is how to understand the current market trend and price movements. The Japanese candlestick chart is one of the most important tools for predicting the short-term moves and making a profit. It is an embodiment of the emotions of fear and greed, which are felt by all traders. Studying the candles will allow you to have insight into the psychology of others who are trading in the market.

While you are taking a risk any time you decide to put money in the stock market, learning to read and interpret the candlestick chart can help to minimize your risk. In the fast-paced world in which we live, changes occur every day. What is popular today may be forgotten next week. The Pet Rock of the '70s hit the scene in a big way, and for a while, almost everyone had a Pet Rock — but, when people lost interest, it quickly disappeared into oblivion.

Now, suppose the Pet Rock had been traded on the stock market. The key to a safe, successful trading experience is knowing when to get in (when the price is low, just before it becomes a household name) and when to get out (when the price is at its peak, just before it begins its downward spiral). Not every stock tumbles into oblivion as quickly as the Pet Rock. Some stocks go up and down as the trends change and as more competition enters the field. Some stocks rise and ebb at a slower pace – and then there are those, like the Pet Rock, that become instant hits and, as soon as the novelty wears off, become instant flops.

The purpose of the candlestick chart is to help you predict the best time to get in and to warn you when the trends are going to change so that you can get out safely while the stock is at or near its peak. The candle line is constructed using basic data about a stock price, much as a Western bar graph — displaying the open, high, low, and closing prices. This means that in order to read the correct signal from a candle line, you must wait for the close of a session, but with this proviso, you will find that candlestick charts are applicable to many different marketplaces, such as regular stock trading, futures and options markets, commodities, and the forex.

If you do not wish to wait until the end of the trading day to get a closing price (daily chart), you can map out a candlestick chart on an hourly basis (intraday chart). This allows you to spot trend reversals even quicker. Candlestick charts cannot be used with tick charts, as tick charts only have closing prices.

The purpose of this book is to help you understand how a candlestick chart is made, how to read the chart and understand the implications of the different patterns, and how to use them to predict when changes will occur. Understanding how to read the trends and changes in the stock market will provide you with a way to minimize your risk and maximize your rate of return. Most, if not all, experts recommend that you do not make your trade on the basis of a candlestick chart alone, but combine the pattern's message with other indicators for confirmation. Some of the more popular indicators used with candlestick charts are discussed later.

Throughout the book, look for the Safety Zone. This is where you will find safety tips to help you invest safely and wisely using the Japanese candlestick charting method. The Safety Zone is designed to go over the principles for safe trading, highlighting the techniques that will preserve your money and opening the possibility for great returns.

As this book is about one particular aspect of trading, I have included only general information on other trading topics, such as the types of orders that you can place with your broker. You should study other material if you need to expand your knowledge on other aspects. That said, I have designed the material to be a thorough introduction to candlestick charting, which requires no previous experience of the technique, and I hope that this introduction will stimulate you to explore the world of candlesticks further.

● **SAFETY ZONE** ●

The most important rule for trading is this: Never trade with money that you cannot afford to lose. Before trading, you should be sure that your personal finances are in order and that you have a solid money management plan. Any time you trade, there is a risk. It is never a good idea to trade with money that is needed for household expenses or to borrow money for trading. Borrowing money to trade will affect the way that you regard the funds and your approach to trading, and you will likely pay a higher interest rate than you will earn from your endeavors — in effect, you will be losing money. It is important to have a healthy monetary portfolio before considering going into the risky world of the stock market.

Never rely on one single method of analyzing the market. The Japanese candlestick chart is the best method for detecting early trend reversals. However, the candlestick chart cannot predict price targets. A price target is the price at which a trader would like to sell in order to realize the most profit. Each trader may have a different price target, dependent upon several factors, such as the cost of the stock when the trader got in, the margin of profit the trader wishes to achieve, and the length of time the trader wishes to stay with the stock. The price target varies per individual trader and depends on the individual's view of the market. Popular methods for determining price targets include pivot highs and lows, trend lines, support and resistance, and moving averages. These can be used in conjunction with the candlestick chart to weigh the risk/reward value of trading.

The History of Candlestick Charting

Candlestick charting is one of the oldest methods used to predict the rise and fall of prices, predating the establishment of the stock market. The patterns of the candlesticks were first analyzed by a wealthy Japanese merchant named Munehisa Homma, or in some citations, Honma, to predict the changing prices of rice — one of the most important commodities in Japan.

During the 1700s, rice was more than just a food in Japan; it was the most precious commodity. People's entire lives revolved around the planting, growing, and harvesting of rice. Not only was rice a staple in the Japanese diet, the straw from dried rice plants was used to make hundreds of everyday items such as hats, clothing, religious figurines, masks, utensils, and decorations.

Rice was essential to the Japanese economy and was traded as much as the American dollar is today. Farmers paid land taxes to the feudal rulers with rice. The rulers then sold the rice from their storehouses. Rice became the currency in Japan during that time.

Munehisa Homma took control of the family rice-trading business in 1750. Each morning, Homma worked in the family warehouse, reconciling the inventory and deliveries that were a part of the day-to-day running of the family business, but his mind was elsewhere.

For 15 years, Homma had been studying ancient records, trying to find a way to decipher the symbols and numbers contained within. He researched over 1,500 years of records. Once Homma began to understand some of the symbols and their meanings in correlation with the numbers presented on the parchments, he began to draw his own charts.

Homma became the first recorded chartist in history. Equipped with this new knowledge, Homma went to the rice market. It was not time for the main growing season, so the big rice merchants were not purchasing the bales of rice the farmers were bringing to market — they were waiting until rice was plentiful and they could buy at lower prices. Homma, however, knew there would be a change in the "trend."

That day, while the other merchants sat around drinking tea and socializing, waiting for the main harvest, Homma quietly purchased all the rice coming in, as well as the rice the farmers would have later in the season. The merchants laughed and thought he must be crazy. They did not understand why he was buying up all the rice when the price would go down as the main crop of rice began coming in. This went on for several days, with Homma continuing to purchase the rice and the merchants scoffing at his impatience.

Then, the tide turned. A messenger arrived at the market and anxiously whispered the news to the leader of the Osaka merchants — the annual rice harvest was ruined due to late, unseasonal rains. Rice would be scarce and prices would soar. With this news, the merchants began to ask the farmers about purchasing their rice — but Homma had already purchased the entire year's crops from every farmer in the area. Homma owned the rice market.

This was just the beginning for Munehisa Homma. Once he had conquered the local market, Homma went on to make over 100 consecutive winning trades. He soon became a financial adviser to the government and was given the highest honor in Japanese custom — the rank of Samurai. Rice became the currency of Japan, and rice coupons became the first form of modern futures.

Homma kept detailed records of his transactions and analyzed the psychology of the market participants using his charts. A book containing his work, *San-en Kinsen Horoku*, was published in 1755 and has formed the basis of Japan's market philosophy. Homma did not invent candlestick charting, but pattern recognition. The charts that Homma drew from his studies became known as candlestick charts and included everything known about prices — the open, high, low, and close. The relationship of each of these four prices with the others determines whether the candlestick is hollow or filled, and Homma gave each pattern its own name.

Homma's candlestick chart became an essential tool in the rice market of Japan. The candlestick chart is still used today by traders because it is the best tool for spotting the emotions that are driving the market. The most common indications are reversal signals, which are patterns that indicate that a price trend is changing, or reversing; there are some continuation signals identifiable with candlesticks, too.

It is important to understand that stock prices rise and fall as a result of several things – the main one being supply and demand. Things such as weather, disasters, and human emotion can also affect prices. For instance, think about crude oil for a moment. Any time a natural disaster occurs, such as Hurricane Katrina, the first thing that happens is panic. Panic results in a change of price for the commodity most affected. In this case, crude oil was affected because of the damage to oil rigs in the Gulf of Mexico.

The candlestick chart is a form of technical analysis that allows you to measure the emotional aspects of the market. Greed, fear, and hope are the most basic emotions associated with trading. Greed can drive prices up, fear can drive prices down, and hope can bring prices up once panic has pushed them down.

Despite this background, candlestick charts have only been known in the West since the 1980s. They were introduced to Western traders by Steve Nison, who wrote the seminal volume *Japanese Candlestick Charting Techniques*, which was originally published in 1991 by the New York Institute of Finance. Before this, Western traders had access to the same information with bar charts, which are explained in the next chapter, but the form of the candlestick is a much more effective visual clue to the emotion of the markets. Following are Steve Nison's comments on the use of candlestick charts.

CASE STUDY: STEVE NISON

Steve Nison, CMT, is president of **candlecharts. com**. As a renowned author and speaker, he has the distinction of introducing candlestick charts to the Western world. Nison wrote three acclaimed books and best-selling DVD workshops. His first book, *Japanese Candlestick Charting Techniques*, is considered the bible of candles and has been translated into over 20 languages.

Regarded as one of the foremost technical analysts in the world, Nison's client list includes Fidelity, J.P. Morgan, Goldman Sachs, Morgan Stanley, NYSE and NASDAQ market makers, hedge funds, and money managers.

His work has been highlighted in *The Wall Street Journal*, *Worth Magazine*, *Institutional Investor*, and *Barron's*. Nison has appeared numerous times on CNBC, and his segment on FNN (the precursor to CNBC) brought in the most viewers that network had ever had.

He has presented his trading strategies in 20 countries to traders from almost every investment firm on how to apply - and profit from - these methods. He has also lectured at numerous universities, and he was invited to speak at the World Bank and the Federal Reserve.

Get Nison's free bi-weekly trading videos and share ideas with fellow traders and Nison at **www.candlecharts.com/free-education/**.

CASE STUDY: STEVE NISON

You are rightly famous in the trading community for introducing candlesticks, and other Japanese charting methods such as kagi, Renko, and three-line break charts to the West. How did you find out about them?

It's amazing, isn't it, that before my work, not one charting package in the Western world had candles? It took years, and much expense, to uncover these "Secrets of the Orient". And it is gratifying to see how it all paid off as attested by the fact every charting platform now has candles.

As to how I discovered candles, in 1987, while I was working as an analyst at a brokerage house, I became acquainted with a Japanese broker. One day, while I was with her in her office, she was looking at one of her Japanese stock chart books (Japanese chart books are in candle form). She exclaimed, "look, a window!" I asked what she was talking about, and she told me that a window was the same as a gap in Western technicals. She went on to explain that while Western technicians use the expression "filling in the gap," the Japanese would say "closing the window." She then used other expressions, like "doji" and "dark cloud cover." I was hooked. I spent the next three years exploring, researching, and analyzing anything I could about candle charts.

As I was reviewing the Japanese books on candles that I was going to have my translator work on, I noticed other kinds of Japanese charts in these books, so I had my translator also work on those sections. These were charts similar to the Western world's point and figure charts, in which there are no dates on the bottom axis. These are the three-line break, Renko, and kagi charts that I revealed in my second book, "Beyond Candlesticks."

In 1996 I started my firm giving trading strategies and education using secret Nison candle strategies and tactics to a small, select group of institutional clients, such as Goldman Sachs, Fidelity Investments, and other top-tier institutions. Recently, I have begun to reveal the very same secret strategies to the public in my live-Web and in-person seminars, in DVD workshops, and on my member site.

CASE STUDY: STEVE NISON

Did you use candlestick charts from the start of your career? If not, how much difference do you think they make to your trades when you learned them?

While I am best known as the Western world's expert on candles, many don't realize I am also an expert in Western technical analysis, since I started using Western technicals in 1974. My former jobs before starting **www.candlecharts.com** were at major brokerage firms, such as Merrill Lynch, giving real-time trade recommendations to the brokers. When I started this, I had not yet done the years of research into candles and was just using Western technical analysis.

When I completed my candle research, I then added my candle strategies into my trade recommendations to the brokers. I quickly became the analyst with the best trading performance for my department, all due to my candle tactics. It was at this point that I knew that since candles pushed me to top trading performance, I could do the same for others through education. In fact, one of my students paid me a great compliment by saying, "Everyone quotes the master, so why not go to the master?"

Do you recommend confirmation of candlestick patterns always, sometimes, or only for particular patterns?

This is a great question, and it brings up an important aspect. Most traders are not aware that recognizing a candle signal is only a small part of correctly using Nison candles. The focus of our education is answering the question, "I see a candle signal; now what do I do?" There could be a candle signal such as a bullish hammer. At times, one should buy on it, and yet another time, one should not do anything with a hammer. So our education starts by helping traders learn how to correctly recognize Nison candles, but then takes them to the next level on what to do next.

I developed my *12 Nison Trading Principles*™ to address what to do next after one sees a candle signal. One of these principles is to add Western technicals to your candle charts. This is because with candles, we are trying to pick early reversals, and to get the odds on our side, we need extra confirmation. Getting confirmation of a Western signal with a candle signal should improve the likelihood of a reversal.

CASE STUDY: STEVE NISON

What other indicators, such as stochastic %D, do you use in conjunction with candlesticks if you want confirmation?

Over the years, I've narrowed down my list to six favorite Western tools. One of them is volume, which shows the force behind the move and therefore complements candle analysis very well because one of the reasons the candles work so well is that they also display the force (or lack of force) behind the recent move. Other tools I focus on are horizontal support and resistance.

Besides indicators, one must also have strong focuses on trade management, such as protective stops, adapting to changing market conditions (what we call being a market chameleon), and setting up a trading journal.

There are many named candlestick patterns. Do you find that you only focus on a few?

Yes. While my books have all the valid candle patterns, my most recent information now focuses on about 13 most common, important candle signals. All the Nison candle signals I have revealed have been refined by generations of use and have been corroborated by at least two separate Japanese sources, either by one of the dozens of books I have had translated from Japanese to English or by a top Japanese institutional trader or analyst.

Nison is rightly regarded as the original Western authority on candlesticks. He still actively teaches, and his Web site, **www.candlecharts.com**, has a great deal of free information; if you cannot find an answer to any candlestick related question here, it is likely that there is no answer. He also offers DVDs and runs courses for those who want to specialize in candlestick pattern recognition. The ease with which a candlestick chart allows you to spot reversal signals in the market has contributed to the growing popularity of the candlestick chart. Since candlestick charts use the same information that Western bar charts use, it is easy to make the transition.

The most common form of analysis in the Western world is the bar graph. The candlestick chart and the bar graph require the same information — the open, high, low, and closing prices of a stock. Since the candlestick chart gives you a broader picture of the market and can be used in combination with most Western technical analysis techniques, the candlestick chart may eventually replace bar charts in the Western world, just as they did in Japan in the 17th century.

The major difference between the two methods is that the candlestick chart provides a more graphic view of the information that will allow you to quickly spot price patterns and other characteristics associated with changes in trend. Being able to spot these reversal signals will help you apply money-management strategies to increase and preserve profits. Most gains or losses occur at the point of a major trend reversal. The ability to spot these reversals allows you to reduce your risk while increasing your return.

Candlestick charts reflect short-term changes within the market. They are almost exclusively the province of the short-term trader rather than the investor, as they have very little to offer to the long-term investor. Candlesticks can be drawn and used on all time frames and are often drawn once for each day of trading. As they are very effective up to about ten time periods, or two weeks if using a daily chart, both swing and day traders have found candlestick charts to be a wonderful addition to their arsenal of market analysis tools.

● SAFETY ZONE ●

The understanding that candlestick charts can bring to the market can seem almost magical at times, and the fact that they have only been discovered in the Western world in recent years is astonishing, given their effectiveness. They derive their power from sound principles in what they show, and from common psychology in application, and they support the traders' argument that trading is an art as well as a science.

From a safety standpoint, you need to realize that they are a tool, but only a tool, that can give some assistance to your trading career. They can only reflect that which is known, providing a window on price history, and are not capable of influencing the future, despite being cited as indicators of it. Your careful study of the topic will allow you to see where the greatest trust in their predictions can be placed and will give you an understanding of their limitations so that you are not vulnerable to misplaced confidence.

2 Introduction to Candlestick Charting

As you have an interest in candlestick charting, you are likely familiar with other charts, and we will consider them briefly as a reminder. A stock price is usually shown on a chart or graph, with price going up and down vertically and time or days going horizontally. The most basic chart has a line going across the chart. When the line goes up, it shows that the price has increased, and when the price declines, the line goes lower.

The axis along the bottom is marked with dates and/or times, depending on the scale chosen. Candlesticks can be used in every time period from minutes to months. A common scale has one candlestick for each day, as this shows short-term trading opportunities. Each candlestick represents a completed session of trading, which means that the prices at the start, or open, and at the end, or close, are needed, as well as the highest and lowest prices that the stock was bought and sold at.

The simple line chart can show you whether a price is increasing or decreasing over time, but that is about all the information available about the trading activity from it. If you are an investor who independently researches the company fundamentals, such as profitability, productivity, and the demand for their products, then the line may be sufficient, giving you the information you need to buy some shares. Looking at the line chart will allow you to see whether your investment is paying off over time.

When you decide to trade — that is, to look for returns on your money in a much shorter time than the years that an investor may hold stocks — you need to become involved with determining how the prices are moving over a shorter duration. Until Nison introduced candlesticks, the standard way of doing this was with price bars — one for each trading period — and the information was assembled into a bar chart. The meaning of the bars is given in the next chapter, and it only includes pricing information.

For a better feel for the market, traders also include other information, either superimposed on the same chart or on a separate chart above or below. Such information includes the amount of shares that were traded in each period, otherwise called the volume. There are many ways of looking at and manipulating the information to produce other factors that can help with trading, and this is generally called "technical analysis."

Charles Dow, who was cofounder of the *Wall Street Journal* and explored moving averages, is attributed with founding technical analysis in the West. He is credited with the Dow Theory, although it was doubtful that he ever assembled his guidelines together, and they were printed in the *Wall Street Journal* as a series of articles authored by him.

Some basics that he annunciated include the idea that a trend will continue unless a significant event stops it. Occasional retrenchments do not disturb that thought. He realized the value of trading volume in confirming trends and that some apparent reversals or hesitations in the trend, may just arise from lack of volume.

His third observation was that there are three fundamental stages to a trend. The first is when not many people have interest in the stock, and the smart money is buying in without being noticed. The second is when other people catch on to the trend and bring it into the public awareness. This leads to the third stage, where the stock gets overbought or oversold when the price comes to a plateau, with clever investors starting to sell.

Dow also ranked the size and strength of market moves, observing that the long-term trends may last for years but may have secondary pullbacks or consolidations. He supported the so-called "efficient market hypothesis," which states that all information is priced into the stock at any time. This is epitomized in the saying, "Buy the rumor, sell the news."

Finally, Dow investigated and commented on relationships between stocks. He always maintained that the Dow Jones Industrial Average and the Dow Jones Transportation Average should move together in a consistent market to confirm the trend, and any deviation between them should be viewed with suspicion. In summary, "what one makes, the other takes," and if transport is not up to carry an apparent increased production, then some fundamental is out of balance. These concepts of Dow Jones are still valid today, and they have been further refined in the development of technical analysis.

Candlestick charts use the same basic information that bar charts use. The significant difference between the two is the way they look at a glance. The construction of the candle line gives a more graphic picture of what is happening in the market. Since the candlestick chart is more graphic, it is easier to read and easier to spot reversal signals that tell you it may be time to make a move or trade. The comparison below shows how the candlestick, or candle line, stands out, versus the ordinary bar line.

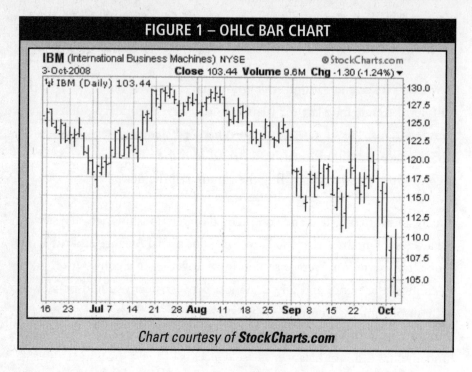

Chart courtesy of *StockCharts.com*

Figure 1 shows the form of charting that was widely used until 20 years ago. Usually called a bar chart, it is actually a Western or OHLC bar chart, where O stands for Open, H for High, L for Low, and C for Close — the four prices that you can find for any completed trading session. While all the information is there, you have to focus on each bar to see what it is telling you.

The time scale along the bottom is based on trading days. The dates shown are the Mondays of the trading weeks, and there are five short lines, or ticks, shown along the bottom for each week. Each day has a bar representing the day's prices.

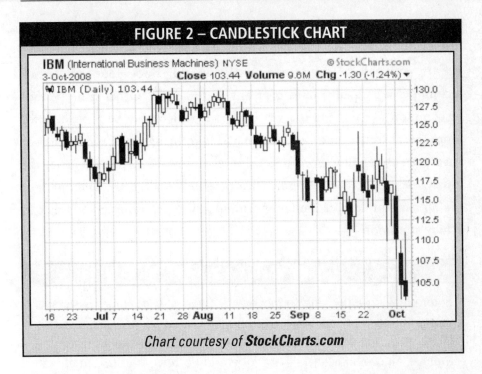

FIGURE 2 – CANDLESTICK CHART

Chart courtesy of StockCharts.com

Compare Figure 1 (OHLC chart) with Figure 2 (candlestick chart), where the price movements are emphasized by the visual effect of the black and white candles. Figure 2 contains exactly the same OHLC information, but more clearly. When you understand the simple construction, whether the price has moved up or down during the session is obvious, as is the range between open and close, and these facts help you in analysis.

As you can see from Figure 2, each candle line resembles a candlestick with a "wick" at each end. Once you learn the basic design of the candlestick chart and the different patterns, you will begin to see how the design can give you a picture of the market at a glance. This picture will provide you with insight into the impact that human emotion is having on the market and will allow you to spot reversal signals at an early stage.

Note that this is a daily chart with the dates shown along the bottom scale and one candle for each day. Candlestick charts can be used for any time period; the only requirement is that you have the four price values of OHLC for each period. The daily chart is mostly used by short-term traders and will be used in examples in this book, but candlestick techniques are equally valid over any time period. Other time periods in common use include the weekly chart, which may be looked at for longer-term trends, and intraday charts, used by day traders, which may have periods ranging from one minute to one hour. In each case, the four values apply. For instance, with the weekly chart, the open price is the opening price on Monday morning, and the closing price is that of Friday afternoon.

● SAFETY ZONE ●

Before making a decision to move on a trade, always compare the risk versus the reward. The reward should always be higher than the risk. If the reward is equal to or lower than the risk, you should not make a move. Since candlestick charts often do not give a price target, you should use a form of analysis that provides this number for you.

The key to making a successful, profitable trade is timing. Using the candlestick chart to spot reversal signals in conjunction with other methods that provide price targets allows you to make a better decision as to the timing of your trade. If you use candlesticks to trigger your trading decisions, then the anticipation of the market that they can provide will open the door to higher profits.

3 Basic Construction of the Candle Line

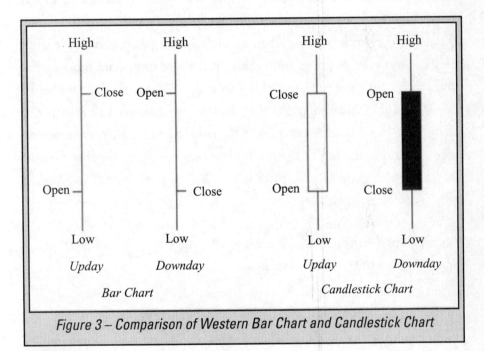

Figure 3 – Comparison of Western Bar Chart and Candlestick Chart

This figure explains in detail the construction of candlesticks together with a comparison to the Western bar chart. The lowest and highest prices reached during the time period are the lower and upper ends of the figures — in this respect, the candlestick and bar charts are similar. The first price of the day's trading is called the "open price," and with the bar chart, it is depicted with a short line to the left of the bar. With a candlestick, it is a horizontal line across the bar. The last price of the day is called the "close," and is a short line to the right of the bar on the bar chart and another horizontal line across with the candlestick.

The information shown in this way completes the bar chart symbol, which is why close examination is needed to understand exactly what happened. With a candlestick, as shown, you have an additional feature — the open and close lines are joined together with a box, which is known as a "real body." The real body is the rectangle that forms the candle of the name. The real body represents the opening and closing prices. Different from the bar chart, the opening and closing prices are interchangeable in the candlestick chart, with the top of the rectangle representing the higher of the two and the bottom representing the lower of the two. For example, if the opening price of a stock is $6, and the closing price is $6.25, the closing price is found at the top of the rectangle. Likewise, if the opening price of a stock is $6, and the closing price is $5.50, the opening price is found at the top of the rectangle.

To clarify the construction of a candle chart, here is a table of daily prices for a week and the equivalent chart.

	Monday	Tuesday	Wednesday	Thursday	Friday
Opening Price	10	10.4	12	13.4	13
Lowest Price during the day	9.6	10	12	11	12
Highest Price during the day	11	12	14	14	13.6
Closing Price	10.8	11.4	13	12	12.6

The feature that sets the candle line apart from other methods and allows the trader to quickly evaluate the information is the color of the real body. Rather than having to compare the top and bottom prices to determine whether the price on top is the opening or closing price, this can be determined by the color of the body. If the rectangle is white, the closing price is represented at the top of the body and the opening price is represented at the bottom. This is called a "white real body." A white real body is usually indicative of a bullish period — the closing price is higher than the opening price, which means the price of the stock grew in value during a specific period; in other words, it was an "upday." If the rectangle is colored in, or black, the opening price is represented at the top of the body while the closing price is represented at the bottom. This is called a "black real body." A black real body is usually indicative of a bearish period in which the closing price is lower than the opening price, which means the stock went down in value for the specified period — a "downday."

For clarity, all candle charts in this book will be shown with this black and white standard, which is the one used most commonly. Another standard used, which you will see sometimes, shows the upday colored green and the downday colored red. Most charting programs allow you to choose any colors you want for the real bodies. Now if you look back at Figures 1 and 2, you can compare exactly how much the candle version of the chart gives you the information at a glance, rather than requiring you to inspect the figure in detail.

The real body represents the opening and closing prices. In order for the candlestick chart to be read properly, the lowest and highest prices of the period must be shown. These are represented by the thin lines above and below the real body — the wicks of the candle. These are known as "shadows." The line found above the body of the candle is the "upper shadow," while the line extending below the body of the candle is the "lower shadow." The highest price of the session is found at the top of the upper shadow, while the lowest price of the session is found at the bottom of the lower shadow.

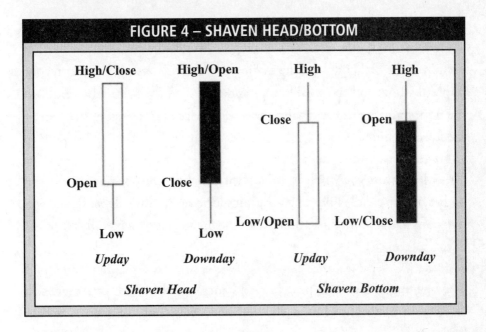

FIGURE 4 – SHAVEN HEAD/BOTTOM

In some instances, the high or low price for the session will match either the open or close price. In this case, the candle may not have a shadow at one end. If the highest price of the session matches the opening or closing price, there will be no upper shadow. This is called a "shaven head." If the lowest price of the session matches the opening or closing price, there will be no lower shadow. This is known as a "shaven bottom."

There are several variations of the real body. We have discussed how the color of the body affects the interpretation of the candle line. Other factors include the length of the real body and of the upper and lower shadows. The length of each will vary according to the range of the prices.

For instance, the larger the range between the opening and closing prices, the longer the body; the larger the range between the price represented at the top of the real body and the highest price of the session, the longer the upper shadow; and the larger the range between the price represented at the bottom of the real body and the lowest price of the session, the longer the lower shadow.

Likewise, the smaller the range between the opening and closing price, the shorter the body; the smaller the range between the price represented at the top of the real body and the highest price of the session, the shorter the upper shadow; and the smaller the range between the price represented at the bottom of the real body and the lowest price of the session, the shorter the lower shadow.

Other indicators you will learn to interpret include the positions of the real bodies on the candle line. The position of the real body is dependent upon the many variables that occur between the open, close, high, and low prices of the session.

The opening and closing prices may be identical, in which case there will be no area to the real body. The real body will simply appear as a thin horizontal line, much the same as the lines in a bar chart. The line will be at the price level of the open and the close. This is a special case candle called a "doji," and its significance will be detailed in the chapters on interpreting the signals.

The opening and closing prices may be the same as the highest and lowest prices of the day, in which case there will be a long real body with no upper or lower shadow — another special case, this time called a "Marubozu." Marubozu means "close-cut" in Japanese, which is an indication that the shadows are close-cut to the body. The color of the real body will indicate which price was highest and which was lowest. The length of the real body depends on the range of the opening and closing prices.

If the opening price is near to the lowest price of the session, the closing price is near to the highest price of the session, and the range between the two is large, this is known as a "long white line." Typically the trader would look for the length of the body to be at least two — and preferably three or more — times the average length seen with this security to qualify as a long body. If the closing price is near to the lowest price of the session, the opening price is near to the highest price of the session, and the range between the two is large, this is known as a "long black line," and similar comments apply to the length.

Both the opening and the closing prices may be close in range and near the highest price of the session, in which case the real body will be small and located at the top of a long lower shadow. In another situation, both the opening and the closing prices may be close in range and near the lowest price of the session, in which case the real body will be small and located at the bottom of a long upper shadow.

If the range between the opening and closing price is small, and the range between the high and low of the session is small, this is represented by a small real body with short upper and lower shadows.

There are many candlestick patterns, and all the patterns have standardized names, some by direct translation from Japanese and some by popular convention, usually following a suggestion from Steve Nison. Some candles appear to be similar in shape and formation, even though they are subject to separate interpretations. The difference usually depends on the situation in which the candle arises, such as whether the market is generally rising or falling.

● SAFETY ZONE ●

The range between the highest and lowest price determines the length of the candle line. Within this candle line, the range between and the actual opening and closing prices determine several things — the length of the real body; the existence of upper and lower shadows, as well as the length of the shadows; and the placement of the real body in the candle line. The shorter the range in price, the shorter the real body and the shadows will be. Likewise, the longer the range in price, the longer the real body and the shadows will be. A longer range in price indicates a session in which the price of the stock has immensely increased or decreased. In order to qualify as a long white line or a long black line, the candle line should be at least three times larger than the real body from the previous session. A long white line is indicative of a bullish market, while a long black line is indicative of a bearish market. However, you should never make a decision based on a long white or black line alone. Since the candlestick charts indicate short-term changes in the market, it is crucial that you always examine the history of the candlestick chart to determine the meaning of a specific line. It is just as important to combine your finding with other technical analysis tools, such as support and resistance, moving averages, and trendlines.

Basic
Trading Strategies

Now that we have covered the basic construction of a candlestick chart, let us consider some basic trading strategies in relation to the charts. The basic strategy for successful trading is being able to determine when to enter and when to exit. In that respect, one of the most important skills a trader can acquire is the ability to recognize trend reversals as early as possible, as a reversal is usually where money is to be made or lost.

Profitable trading involves several factors, the most important of which are emotional control and money management. Trading with their own money makes many people uncomfortable and unable to assess their position intellectually, and allowing emotions to control one's actions is usually not good for trading profits.

Taking the correct position on money management can make or break a novice trader. It is usually recommended that you risk no more than 2 percent of your trading capital on any one trade. This does not mean that you only use 2 percent to buy a stock, just that you should work out, before you ever enter the trade, at what price you are going to sell and take a loss if the trade goes against you, and you can work out backwards how much money you can afford to put into a particular position to satisfy this guideline.

Although trading uses technical analysis to determine the stocks to buy and sell, many people refer to fundamental analysis when looking to invest long term, as fundamental analysis concentrates on the underlying value of a company, how well it is run, whether sales are good and improving, and other things that matter in the long run. Technical analysis, on the other hand, does not bother much with the actual underlying value of a stock as determined by fundamental analysis. Instead, technical analysis considers how a stock is viewed by other traders, and this is determined by the actions of the other traders in the marketplace. Successful trading is about finding stocks that will change price in a short period of time and anticipating the actions of others by determining their emotions and sentiment. Fundamental analysis has little to do with this, as the management and accounts of a company do not usually vary much in a short time.

Once you learn to set up a candlestick chart and interpret the lines and patterns represented, you will learn to spot trend reversals much more quickly than is possible with bar charts. Combining these skills with the information gathered from other analysis tools will allow you to make successful trades with less risk. This, in turn, will allow you to see higher rates of return as you increase your profits by learning when to buy (when the price is low) and when to sell (when the price is high). Honing in on your skills using the candlestick charting method of spotting early trend reversals will allow you to get in as early as possible and to get out as close to the peak as possible.

It is important to note that no matter how good you become at reading and interpreting candlestick charts, you will seldom want to initiate a trade on the basis of the candles alone. In his case study included earlier, Steve Nison emphasizes the need for some sort of confirmation. There is a general description in this book of some other common chart indicators following the candle pattern section, and it is wise to use these to have some confirmation before acting. The indicators included are ones that have been used by the experts contributing their case studies to this book, so you can be assured that they are indicators that work well with candlestick charts. Some confirmation of a trading opportunity can be found by waiting until at least one period has passed and seeing whether the price has started in the expected direction. Occasionally, this could be considered sufficient evidence to enter a trade.

If you have not done much trading before, you may be disappointed to hear that you will have losing trades, even though you are studying this book. The perfect trading system or strategy has never been invented. Your profit comes from making more than you lose, and that is one reason why you need good money management — to minimize your losses. The market is bigger than any player and will do what it wants. Learning to observe and accept what it does, rather than dwelling on what it "ought to" do, will help tremendously in your trading career.

Later, I talk about the importance of having a trading plan, which is about knowing what you will do in any situation, from entering a trade through to when you exit the trade, whether it was successful or not. The power of emotions is also a factor, and unless you have a clear idea before you start trading how you are going to do it, you will probably make mistakes due to your emotions, particularly fear and greed.

Remember that there is no perfect trading strategy, and that the market will sometimes do the strangest things. No one can predict with certainty what will happen, and that is why you must have a fallback position ready if things do not turn out well. You will need to know how far you can let a price slide in the wrong direction before you call it a day and close the trade at a loss, and you must condition yourself to not think twice when you reach that point. It is much harder to take a loss if you have let the price drift down further in the hope that it would come back.

For successful trading, you need to become familiar with three basic aspects of technical analysis — candlestick reversal patterns, moving averages, and volume. You can add an oscillator for further indication, and most traders do, as you can see from the case studies throughout the book. However, you also want to avoid "analysis paralysis," where you have so many different indicators that you can always find a reason for not making a trade, and you avoid the hard task of deciding where to put your money.

Decide which indicators you are going to use, paper trade with them until you are satisfied, then just stick with them for your active trading. As part of your continuing education, investigate alternative indicators and other strategies by reading and by paper trading them, but do not confuse your live account with your research efforts. Once you have identified, and proven by back-testing, an improvement to your trading plan, document it and start using it, but not until you have developed the confidence in it that you had in your first plan.

● SAFETY ZONE ●

Candlestick patterns are a very powerful, informative tool that provides an earlier indication of price reversals than conventional technical indicators, which often lag the price movements. They provide an idea of the way investors are viewing the market at any particular time.

While quite useful, you must recognize their limitations. Candlestick charts should be used with other technical indicators from Western analysis to provide stronger indications and confirmation of the anticipated moves.

Your trading should always allow for the certainty that some trades will not work as expected, and you should study general trading strategies to reinforce the correct way to preserve and enhance your capital. The most important notion you should bear in mind in regard to your money is not how to make more quickly, but how to preserve what you have indefinitely. In that way, your trading approach will be a winning one.

The Psychology of the Candles

Before going into detail on the actual patterns that are recognized and used, I would like to explain the basics of the psychology used. Trading is an art as well as a science, and purely understanding numbers is not sufficient to be successful. With short-term trading, your gain is someone else's loss — for the most part — as fundamentals of a stock do not usually change much in the short-term. Because there is no change in the overall amount, this is called a zero-sum game, where no additional money enters the arena, but money is just traded backward and forward.

Therefore, it is basically a battle of wits between you and many other traders. Most people who start trading lose money and give up within six months. This is not so hard to understand for a zero-sum game, as there are also costs associated with your trading setup and with trading itself. If your goal is to make a consistent, long-term profit, then you need to ensure that you are trading smarter than the majority.

While this would discourage many would-be traders who lack the foundation, skills, or disposition to make a success of it, this should not deter you, but should cheer you up. As there is always a ready supply of novice traders making their moves in the market, with commitment and training, you will be able to outwit them and make money on a regular basis.

The variations that you can have with a single candle are limited in concept, although potentially infinite in precise numbers. The concepts are the important part; it does not matter whether the closing price is 56.180 or 56.190 so much as whether this is close to the opening price or far away — a "long black line" or a "long white line."

After explaining the established candle patterns and their interpretations, I discuss how they are used and the significant features to bear in mind when trying to be a successful trader. The list of recognized patterns is extensive, and you will find repeated ideas that, if you assimilate them, will enable you to start reading the candlestick charts effectively for yourself. You should not expect to learn all these patterns at once, if ever, but should just examine and think about what is being expressed in the candles.

The Doji

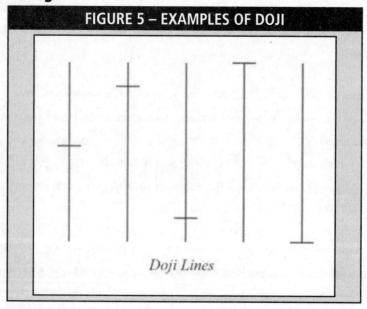

FIGURE 5 – EXAMPLES OF DOJI

Doji Lines

One of the most important styles of candle is the doji, as shown in Figure 5. The Japanese regard this candle as extremely significant. The true doji has no height to the real body, showing that the opening and closing prices were the same. Sometimes in pattern interpretation, you will also allow a very small body in place of the doji, as the principle is similar. The dash that is the real body can be anywhere along the length of the shadows, even at the top, showing that the open, close, and highest prices of the session were all the same; or it can be at the bottom, which means that the open, close, and lowest values of the session were identical. Although not pictured here, the shadow length will vary, and this too is a factor in interpretation.

The usual meaning given to this candle is that the market is undecided, not knowing whether to go up or down and finishing up where it started. If the buyers were keener than the sellers, giving you a bull market, the price would increase over the day — one by one, the buyers would in effect say, "Yes, we will pay a little more to get this stock," and the price would move upward. If there was selling pressure in a bear market, the price would similarly creep lower over time.

In summary, the potential sellers and potential buyers are in balance at this time and price. That is why this is often considered a point at which the current trend in the price can reverse, making it a trading opportunity. This indication is considered to be stronger when the doji comes in an upward rally in price. A doji that comes in a rallying market is called a Northern Doji to emphasize its position at the top.

Trading volume is often a factor in determining the implications of a particular type of candlestick, and volume tends to be greater when there is an uptrend. With so many trades, it is difficult for a doji, to be achieved in a rally, which may be a partial explanation of its extra significance.

When a doji comes in a falling trend, it does not necessarily indicate a reversal. Quite often, the doji, which tends to mean that the market is undecided about the value, just represents a resting place in a market plunge rather than an optimistic turnaround. If you were to view the volume of trading, you might find a rest from trading is literally what is happening with a low number of trades. The doji in a decline is called a Southern Doji to distinguish it from the Northern Doji.

The Spinning Top

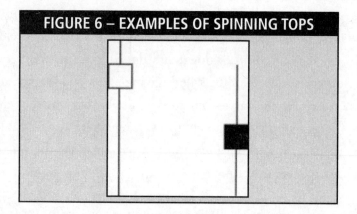

FIGURE 6 – EXAMPLES OF SPINNING TOPS

The spinning top is characterized by a short real body. It is similar in meaning to a doji in that the short body indicates that neither the buyers nor the sellers are actually in control of the market, although it is not quite so balanced. A spinning top can be significant in a price pattern, even though a single spinning top in a trading range may mean nothing special.

When you are determining whether a candle is a spinning top, you need to compare the real body length to the typical candle body length. The shortness is relative, and if the chart for a particular stock does not have very long bodies normally, then to be significant, the spinning top body would need to be much shorter. While some signs are clear, other candlesticks may require subjective interpretation. This is where practice and experience can help you make the correct decision.

The spinning top may come after a long rally or fall in price, and the usual interpretation is that the trend is losing steam. That may be an indication of the fight between buyers and sellers becoming more balanced. As with most candle interpretations, you would normally look for other indications before taking any trading action.

High Wave Candle

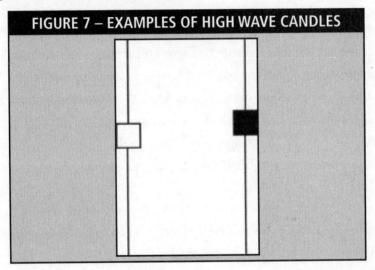

FIGURE 7 – EXAMPLES OF HIGH WAVE CANDLES

A subset of the spinning top is called the high wave candle. To qualify as a high wave candle, the spinning top needs to have long shadows, both upper and lower. This is an even more indecisive indication, for both the buyers and sellers have explored a large price range during the trading period, pushing out to the limits of the shadows, only to settle back to near where the price started out. The market is truly confused as to where the price should be.

The Long Body

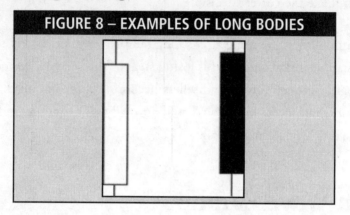

FIGURE 8 – EXAMPLES OF LONG BODIES

At the opposite end of the spectrum from the doji, the long-bodied candlesticks are shown in Figure 8. These are taken to show a strong bullish interest for the long white line or a strong bearish interest for the long black line in a particular stock or security. Often, these will form part of a price pattern on a candlestick chart, and they are a significant indicator. A particular case of the long-bodied lines is the Marubozu, mentioned previously, which has neither upper nor lower shadows.

The length of the body is again relative to the normal length that you can see on the chart and must be noticeably different, perhaps three times as long as the previous day's candlestick. The long bodies are particularly interesting when they penetrate through a value that had previously been the limit of the price.

The "support line" can be drawn underneath the previous low prices and is the temporary limit for where you expect the prices to go. The "resistance line" is drawn above the highs that the price is currently hitting and is the upward limit, for the time being, of the price movement. The area between the support and resistance is the current "range" of the stock, and you will often see the price bounce back and forth in this limited range for a period of time.

When a price makes a definite move through one of these lines, it is called a "breakout." A breakout can lead to the price moving significantly and establishing another range at a higher or lower level. If a long line breaks through the range boundaries, this is a strong indication that the change is well supported by the market and that the breakout will come about and hold.

This has covered the different lengths of the real body, but there can be variation in the shadow lengths. If you have a long shadow, it suggests that the market tried to get to a different level, but the values were rejected before the close. Therefore, the long shadow often suggests that there is insufficient support in the direction moved.

There are many ways in which these basic shapes combine to form candlestick patterns, and the interpretations are given on the following pages. Candlestick patterns can comprise as little as one candlestick, although it is normal to consider the general trend, if not the specific candles, when coming to a conclusion about what the candlestick may mean. Often, a candle pattern can be inverted and used with the opposite meaning, as you will see.

In this regard, you should note that a chart can have three possible directions — up, down, and sideways. It is easy to think that if a stock is not trending upward, it must be trending downward, but that is not the case. Many stocks go sideways for a significant period of time.

When a stock goes sideways, that does not mean that the price does not vary at all. The fluctuations in the price tend to center around a particular value and stay within the range. Some traders trade when a stock is range-bound, buying at the low end of the range and selling at the high for small, repeatable gains. In the diagrams in the following chapters, where the trend before the pattern is important, it is indicated by an arrow sloping up or down. The reversal and continuation patterns only make sense in the context of a trending stock price.

You will also note that some signals mean more if they are coincident to an increase in trading volume. Volume can be an important additional factor to add to the significance of any particular pattern, and even for the regular candlestick patterns, you need to be sure that the signal is relevant by verifying that it was not based on an unusually low volume. As a general guide, when the trend is upward, you can expect the volume to be strong; in a downtrend, there may be less trading volume.

● SAFETY ZONE ●

In order to use candlestick charting successfully, you need to understand the psychology of trading. This is not only the way that other traders are reacting and moving the markets, but also the influence of greed and fear on your own actions.

Until traders use their own money, they do not realize how much these emotions can affect them. Suffice to say, most traders find that conquering their emotions is one of the major challenges they face, and it is part of the reason that you may expect to trade better after several months, rather than when you first start.

When you look at the candlestick signals, remember that most should be confirmed with other charting indicators before entering a trade. You should take as much information as you need to make a valued judgment on when to trade. This does not mean that you need to overanalyze any situation, but you must be selective and choose complimentary factors which, when they align, will give you confirmation of a likely profit.

6 Candlestick Patterns — Single-Day Reversal Signals

The single-day reversal signals apply when a stock is trending. You can regard the single candles as the basic building blocks that indicate traders' overall sentiments. As they are only single candles, their interpretation is limited, and you will see in the next chapters how these fundamental units can be combined with others to give more detailed and sometimes more definite, signals. In trading, nothing is certain, but you can learn how to stack the odds in your favor by learning what each candlestick implies.

Long-Legged Doji

General Pattern

The Long-Legged Doji appears in the middle of the trading session and is a doji with long upper and lower shadows, or "long legs."

Meaning

While a doji shows that there is indecision, and that neither the buyers nor the sellers have sufficient control to move the closing price away from the opening price, the Long-Legged Doji exemplifies this feeling. The long shadows are evidence of significant activity pushing the price first one way and then the other, but without any lasting effect. The Long-Legged Doji thus represents massive indecision in the market — the price soared, then dropped drastically and evened out at the close of the session, or the price dropped drastically, then soared and evened out at the close of the session.

Four-Price Doji

General Pattern

The Four-Price Doji is a rare occurrence. The only time you will see a Four-Price Doji is when all four prices — open, close, high, and low — are the same for the trading session. This only results if there has been no price movement over the time period.

Meaning

In many cases, the Four-Price Doji occurs because of a lack of data. The first check you should do is on the trading volume. However, if a true Four-Price Doji occurs, it indicates a complete and total uncertainty in the market — neither the bears nor the bulls have any clue as to which direction this market will turn.

Dragonfly Doji

General Pattern

As you can see by the diagram, the Dragonfly Doji is represented by an open and close price that is near to or at the high of the trading session. The long lower shadow indicates that the market fell during the trading session. However, since the closing price is the same as the opening price, the price was pushed back up. The Dragonfly Doji may be seen in an uptrend or a downtrend.

Meaning

A doji during a decline is usually not an important indicator; however, the exception is the Dragonfly Doji, which can represent a turning point for the market. The Dragonfly Doji best represents a bullish turning point, as the price drops during trading, but buyers push the price back up before the close of the session. You can also view this as the bears trying to make the price lower, but it does not stick, indicating that the bears are weak and cannot have their way.

Unless there are many doji in a chart, a doji should always make you pay attention to what the market is doing. While it may just be a low activity day, or a time when the traders stand back and take stock of their position, it can signal a reversal, and you should check other indicators to see whether the current mood of the market would support that action.

Hammer

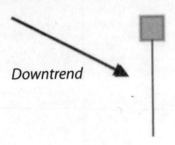

Downtrend

General Pattern

The Hammer has a small real body at the top of the candlestick. It can be white or black, so is shown as grey above. It might have a very short upper shadow but no more than 10 percent of the total range of the candle. The lower shadow should be two or three times the length of the body. It occurs in a downtrend, and the name "Hammer" is said to stand for the market hammering out the bottom to the price.

The indication of a reversal would be stronger the shorter the real body is and the longer the lower shadow. A white body would also increase the force of signal.

Meaning

As the Hammer is very comparable to the Dragonfly Doji, discussed in the previous section, the meaning is similar. The market is bearish, and more selling takes place on this day, lowering the price. However, the market does not keep up the selling pressure, and the price returns to near the opening price by the close. When traders see that the bears are not maintaining their impetus, they may be afraid for their own bearish stance and expect that the bulls are about to start the price increasing. This would be confirmed by a higher opening price on the next day.

Hanging Man

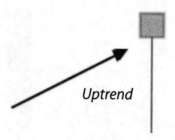

Uptrend

General Pattern

The Hanging Man has a small real body at the top of the candlestick. It can be white or black, so is shown grey above. In this respect, it can be identical to the Hammer pattern, as seen above. The difference is that it comes in an uptrend. Again, it is allowed to have a very short upper shadow and still be counted as a valid pattern. The lower shadow should be a minimum of two times the length of the body. The name Hanging Man, which is translated from the Japanese name *kanzuchi* for this figure, is supposed to derive from this candle looking like a hanging man.

The stronger version of this candle pattern would have a shorter real body; shorter upper shadow, if any; a long lower shadow; and a black body. In this respect, it becomes closer to the Dragonfly Doji, also a sign of a possible reversal.

Meaning

In this case, the previous market sentiment has been bullish. For this pattern to form, the price must drop during the day to much lower than the open, but rally back up before the close. The indication is that this may be the start of a sell-off, even though the lower prices did not stick on this day. Look for confirmation of the market opening lower the next day.

Bearish Belt Hold

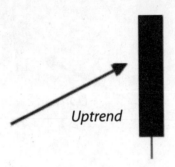

Uptrend

General Pattern

The Bearish Belt Hold is a black or bearish candlestick with a long real body. It has a shaven head and only a small lower shadow. Lack of the shadow on the top is one of the characteristics of the pattern. The name "Belt Hold" was given to it by Steve Nison, and the Japanese name, *yorikiri*, meaning "to push out."

Compare this to the Hanging Man in the previous section. There is no indecision shown in that pattern by a long lower shadow, which is the characteristic of the doji and short body patterns. Instead, there is a definite decision of the market to lower the price during the trading period, with a long black body.

Meaning

The Bearish Belt Hold opens at the highest price of the day, which is also a gap up above the previous day's prices. From there, the price only falls, with the close near to the lowest price of the day.

As the price is falling from the start of trading, there is general concern among the traders who pile in to unload their shares, creating the bearish move that they fear.

Gravestone Doji

General Pattern

In one sense, being a doji, the Gravestone Doji is in ways very similar, and thus, the herald of uncertainty in the market. The Gravestone Doji, called *tohba* by the Japanese, appears when the open and close price is the same as the low price of the trading session.

Meaning

The Gravestone Doji is the opposite of the Dragonfly Doji and represents a bearish market sympathy. The Gravestone Doji indicates that, during the trading session, the price rises drastically and then falls back to the original opening price, which is the low of the session. This shows that the bulls are not strong enough to establish or maintain a rally. Thus, the strongest interpretation is when the Gravestone Doji comes in an uptrend, which indicates that the trend may be ready to reverse.

The Hammer pattern, covered just a few pages ago, and the Shooting Star, which we will cover next, are two of the favorite patterns of David Jenyns, an Australian trader and entrepreneur, who submitted this case study.

CASE STUDY: DAVID JENYNS

Jenyns is recognized as a leading expert on both MetaStock and profitable trading system design. He earned this title after working at Ord Minnett (one of Australia's top brokerage firms) and training hundreds of traders at HomeTrader, Australia's leading stock market education company.

Jenyns has written numerous best-selling trading books and courses, including: *Triple Your Trading Profits Workshop*, *The MetaStock Programming Study Guide*, *The MetaStock Secrets Seminar DVD*, *Trading Secrets Revealed*, *Ultimate Trading Systems*, and *Free Trading Systems*.

Jenyns' tips and advice on trading have been featured in many trading journals and magazines, including the Australian Financial Review, Chartpoint, Smart Investor, Your Trading Edge, Short-Term Trading, and the Guppytraders newsletter.

Download Jenyns' free trading methods at **www.freetradingsystems.org**, or keep up to date with his most recent material by visiting his blog, at **www.davidjenyns.com**.

What type of trading do you use candlesticks with — what markets and time periods?

I tend to use candlesticks with shorter-term trading, typically trades lasting less than 20 days. I find candlesticks are best used to provide an insight into the psychology/sentiment of a market. As a result, I generally use them as the trigger for my entry.

Contracts for difference (CFDs) are more suited to shorter-term trading, because of their leveraged nature, and are therefore well suited to candlesticks. I sometimes use candlestick analysis for equities trading; however, I've found candlesticks to be less relevant as your trading time stretches out. That is to say, the longer you hold onto a trade, the less important timing your entry point becomes.

CASE STUDY: DAVID JENYNS

When and how did you start getting interested in trading?

I first got interested in trading in the late 1990s. I was still in high school and had a friend who would constantly brag to me about how well he was doing in the markets. In hindsight, I suspect he was just telling me about his winning trades, but that was enough to get me hooked.

After I finished high school, I took out a $5,000 loan to do a trading course. Luckily, it turned out to be a great course, mainly because of the caliber of the presenters involved. Not all courses are like that. I definitely got my money's worth, and I haven't looked back since.

Did you use candlestick charts from the start of your trading? If not, how much difference do you think they made to your trades when you learned to interpret them?

The course I attended talked quite a bit about candlesticks, so yes; I have used them from the beginning of my trading career. I was instantly attracted to them because they are visually so powerful. I have tried other charts, such as bar, line and point, and figure charts, but none of them quite match up to the visual impact of candlesticks; none are as effective or easy to work with.

Do you enter a trade on the basis of a candlestick pattern only — always, sometimes, or never?

I never enter a trade based on a candlestick pattern alone.

I always like to trade in the direction of the underlying trend. Accordingly, I have a set of criteria I like a trading candidate to exhibit before entering, and candlesticks are just part of this setup. I look for the underlying trend direction and identify a candlestick reversal pattern.

I only use these candlestick reversal patterns to enter a position, never to exit.

CASE STUDY: DAVID JENYNS

What other indicators do you use in conjunction with candlesticks if you want confirmation? Which do you find work best in combination with candle signals?

I find that candlesticks are most useful as an entry signal. I always look at other underlying conditions in conjunction with the candlesticks (see next answer).

Do you find filters, such as price or volume, effective in assisting selection of worthwhile candlestick patterns?

I look for a number of other underlying conditions that a trading candidate must exhibit before I use candlesticks as my entry trigger.

The three categories of underlying conditions I watch are trend, volume, and volatility.

In terms of trend, I just do some basic analysis looking for a shorter-term moving average above a longer-term moving average. I also like to see an increase in the average volume. In an ideal situation, volume is higher than average for bullish candles and lower for bearish ones. In terms of volatility, I like the trading candidate to have a minimum of 3 percent volatility.

There are many named candlestick patterns. Do you find that you only focus on a few, and if so, which?

There are too many named candlestick patterns for my liking. Fortunately, since I use candlesticks for my entry signal rather than my exit, I just focus on reversal patterns. My favorite ones being the Shooting Star, the Hammer, and engulfing patterns (Engulfing Bull and Engulfing Bear). All those patterns indicate a turning point in the trend.

Again, I wouldn't act on a candlestick analysis alone.

Shooting Star

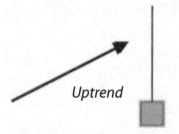

Uptrend

General Pattern

The Shooting Star comes in an uptrend and is not considered a strong reversal signal. It can have either color of body, although a black body would give a stronger indication of the impending reversal. It is called a Shooting Star because of its appearance, and the upper shadow should be at least three times the length of the real body.

Usually, the Shooting Star requires the open to be gapped up from the previous day. There is an attempt at a rally, which fails, and the close is down near the open. Compare this pattern to the previous Gravestone Doji to see the similarities.

Meaning

As the rally fails, and particularly if it is after a bullish gap open, the implication is that the sentiment is starting to turn bearish. This may lead to traders selling their long positions, which would contribute to a reversal. This should be checked against the next day's trading, when a lower opening price would confirm the trend.

Inverted Hammer

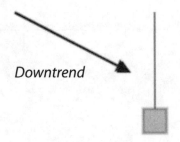

Downtrend

General Pattern

The Inverted Hammer is similar in form to the Shooting Star but comes in a downtrend, rather than an uptrend. It has a similar meaning to the Hammer and signals a reversal at the bottom of a downtrend. The Inverted Hammer, as its name suggests, is an upside-down Hammer. It has a short real body at the bottom of the candlestick, and the upper shadow should be about two times as long as the body. There should be no lower shadow. The real body can be either color, but a white body helps strengthen the indication.

Meaning

The day usually opens with a downward gap, in line with the established trend. The stock rallies during the day against the trend, but the rally does not stick, and the closing price is down near the opening price. The indication is that the bulls want to take over the trading, but they were not quite strong enough on this day.

The next day will help confirm or deny the reversal pattern, if the next day trades up, then a reversal should follow. The long upper shadow that fails to hold can, in certain circumstances, show that the bulls are giving way. You need to look for confirmation that the bulls are strengthening, either with technical indicators showing that the stock is oversold and ready to rise or by waiting for the next day or two of pricing.

Bullish Belt Hold

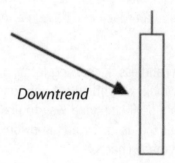

Downtrend

General Pattern

Finally, the Bullish Belt Hold is a white or bullish candlestick with a long real body. It has a shaven bottom and only a small upper shadow. Lack of the shadow on the bottom is one of the characteristics of the pattern. It comes in a downtrend, and at the open, there is a gap in price below the previous candles.

Meaning

The drop in price is immediately followed by a rise in price, which runs counter to the current trend. As a result of this movement, many short positions are covered, and the buying turns the trend around. Compare this to the preceding Inverted Hammer pattern. The long white body of the Bullish Belt Hold shows a bullish sentiment; the Inverted Hammer's short body implies uncertainty, and thus, it may be interpreted as a time of possible change. In either case, the implication for future price movement is the same.

● SAFETY ZONE ●

The fundamentals of candlestick analysis depend on a thorough understanding of each of these single-candle forms, and the market moves that form them. With the exception of knowing exactly at what time of day each trade occurred — which would probably be an impossible amount of information to assimilate and of no real value — the candlesticks can give you all the information that you could possibly need about the approach and mental attitude of fellow market participants.

Some traders use the candlestick charting forms but do not refer to the named patterns. This makes it difficult if you want to discuss a trade with another, but it is a perfectly good way to play the market. It is the meaning of the candles that is important, and you will develop a feeling for this after studying many charts.

Candlestick Patterns — Two-Day Reversal Signals

These two-day candle patterns combine the basic candlesticks with which you have become familiar and express the reversal signal more explicitly, in many cases. However, it is still often necessary to proceed with caution and consider other factors before committing a trade — sometimes, a similar pattern can have a totally different interpretation, depending on whether the stock is oversold or overbought, as determined by technical indicators. The previous trend is almost always important in determining the appropriate understanding.

Bearish Engulfing

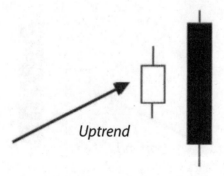

Uptrend

General Pattern

The engulfing patterns are very common and consist of two candlesticks of opposite color. The Bearish Engulfing has a large black (bearish) candlestick on the second day whose real body completely covers, or engulfs, the previous small white real body.

The shadows do not matter in identifying this pattern. What matters is that it comes in an uptrend, and the top of the bearish candle is as high as or higher than the top of the white, and the bottom is as low as or lower than the bottom of the white real body.

The tops or bottoms may be the same but not both. The pattern is stronger when the difference in body size is larger and also when the shadows of the first candle are engulfed.

Meaning

This is an uptrend that is slowing. The small white body indicates the loss of momentum and is usually on small volume. In contrast, the engulfing body has a high volume. On the engulfing day, the open is at a new high, but it is not sustained. The traders rush to sell off their holdings, creating the large volume and the long candlestick. When the third day opens lower, that tends to confirm the pattern.

Dark Cloud Cover

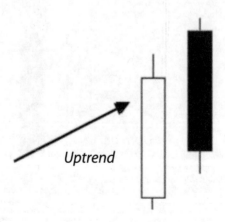

Uptrend

General Pattern

A long white day is followed by a long black day. This pattern is different from the Bearish Engulfing pattern in that the first white candle is longer. The opening price on the second day is gapped up above the high of the first day, but despite this bullish move, the day trades lower and lower through the period and finishes well down into the real body of the previous day. To be a Dark Cloud Cover, it must fall below the midpoint of the long white day. Note that it does not fall below the real body; otherwise, it would be a Bearish Engulfing pattern.

Meaning

The Dark Cloud Cover is well named, due to the image as well as the effect on traders. This pattern has a counterpart in the opposite Piercing Line pattern, covered later, which is a bullish reversal. The Dark Cloud Cover indicates that a bearish reversal is likely. The bearish tendency throughout the day makes the previously bullish traders think twice about the trend.

Bearish Meeting (Counterattack) Line

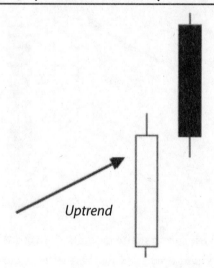

Uptrend

General Pattern

The Bearish Meeting Line pattern is two long candles of opposite colors. Coming in an uptrend, the Bearish Meeting Line starts with a white, bullish candle, followed by a black, bearish candle. The term 'meeting line' refers to the fact that both candles have the same closing price. On the second day, there is a big jump in the opening price, but the market pulls back to the close. Compare this with the similar Dark Cloud Cover, preceding.

Meaning

The trend is continued strongly during the first day, and there is a large gap on the second day. The trend is completely ignored by the subsequent trading activity, and the close at the same price is a good indication that the trend has reversed, which would be supported by a lower open on the next day. This pattern is not considered as strong as the Dark Cloud Cover, perhaps due to the second candle being at a higher price level, which runs counter to the implication of reversal.

One Black Crow

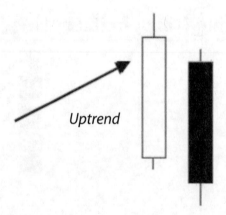

Uptrend

General Pattern

This pattern starts with a long white day in an uptrend. The second day has a long black body, which opens below the previous close, and closes down further, below the first day's opening price.

Meaning

The first day suggests that the trend, in this case bullish, is continuing. Therefore, when the second day happens as described, this is an interruption to the trend and shows the possibility of a reversal. The opening price of the second day is lower than the previous close, and the day is a down day, so both these facts point to a bearish trend starting. Frequently, the advice is to see what the next day shows to confirm the turn down, and the One Black Crow pattern alerts you to watch this particular stock closely when it continues trading.

Bearish Kicking

General Pattern

The Bearish Kicking pattern, also called the Kicker, is another combination of a bull candle followed by a bear candle. In this case, the second, bearish candle is fully lower than the first, and both candles are Marubozu, or at least have very small shadows. Unlike most of the patterns in this section, this pattern does not have to be in an uptrend. The gap defines this pattern.

Meaning

The first candle is again an indication that there is good support for the price that it will go higher. The second opens below any price traded on the first day and carries on sinking, which shows strong bearish sentiment. The absence of shadows suggests that the sentiment is generally agreed by the traders, with little argument.

This pattern is unusual, and is perhaps the strongest indicator there is for a downtrend to take place. There may be a particular reason for the occurrence of the Kicker, such as some after-hours news of a contract cancellation, a fraud allegation, or another matter that fundamentally changes the way that the company is viewed.

Bearish Harami

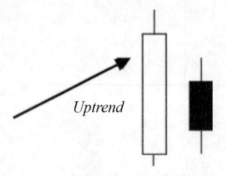

Uptrend

General Pattern

The Harami consists of two candles, the real body of the second one being fully contained within the real body of the first. Compare this to the engulfing pattern, where the second candle engulfs the first. Harami is actually Japanese for *pregnant*, and the candle pattern resembles the side view of a pregnant woman.

The Bearish Harami starts with a long white candle in an uptrend, and the second candle is shorter and contained within the body of the first. The lengths of the shadows are not considered significant.

Meaning

The Bearish Harami starts with a long day in the direction of the current trend. The second day starts lower and only trades in a small range, closing lower still. This indicates that the trend may be failing, and if the trading volume is low on the second day, that is a further indication that a reversal may be coming. The trend showing signs of weakening causes traders to consider selling their holdings, supporting the reversal.

Bearish Harami Cross

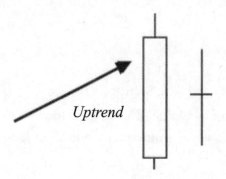

Uptrend

General Pattern

As you can see, the Bearish Harami Cross is a development from the simple Harami. Instead of a black body in the second position, there is a doji. The doji is within the real body of the first candlestick. This pattern comes in a trending market.

Meaning

The doji always means some sort of uncertainty, as neither the bulls nor the bears has enough control to change the closing price. As with the Harami, this pattern denotes a time of indecision, and having a doji rather than a short body strengthens that message. One may well expect a low volume on the second day, which emphasizes how the trading is paralyzed at the current price level with the bulls losing their power.

Bearish Doji Star

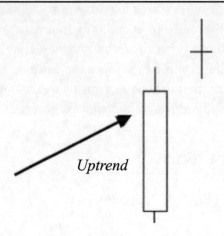

Uptrend

General Pattern

Similar to the Harami Cross, the Bearish Doji Star is a long white day, followed by a gap up — typical of a Star formation — to a second-day doji. The doji has moderate price movement, but is not long-legged.

Meaning

As with the previous pattern, the presence of a doji candle is a powerful indicator of uncertainty, which suggests that the trend may be ending, followed by a reversal. The uptrend is supported firmly by the first candlestick, and the gap upward seems to enforce the mood.

The failure of the trading during the second day to close any higher, though, casts serious doubt on the underlying strength. The reversal will be confirmed when the next day opens at a lower price.

Descending Hawk

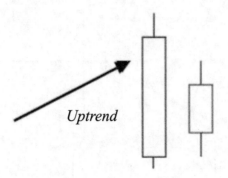

Uptrend

General Pattern

Similar to the Harami but with both real bodies the same color, the Descending Hawk comes in an uptrend. The real body of the second day is wholly contained in the first day's long white body.

Meaning

The Descending Hawk is a bearish reversal signal. The first long white day continues the current uptrend, but prices open lower on the second day. The volume may be subdued, and the size of the real body is reduced, although the closing price is still higher than the open. This may give a clue of reversal but is best confirmed by the next candlestick, which would be lower and may close below the first day's real body for the pattern to be a valid reversal signal.

Matching High

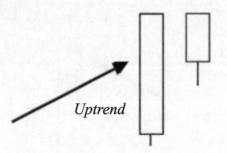

Uptrend

General Pattern

The Matching High pattern arises in an uptrend and consists of two white candles. Both candles have the same closing price, or top of body, and have shaven or nearly shaven heads.

Meaning

The first day confirms the uptrend, but the second day, although opening higher than the previous day did, cannot go above the price level already reached. This is a classic indication that the resistance level for the price, at least for the short-term, has been reached. While both candles are bullish, allowing the trend to continue upward, the fact that the levels are the same is psychologically significant. Any further candles that do not exceed that level provide more confirmation, and you may also look for prices falling as confirmation.

Last Engulfing Day Top

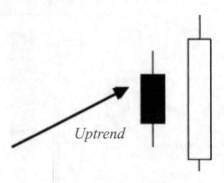

Uptrend

General Pattern

The Last Engulfing Day Top comes in an uptrend and consists of a small bodied black candle on the first day and a large white body on the second day. The large white body engulfs the first day, with the bottom of the body lower and the top of the body higher than the previous one.

Meaning

The Last Engulfing Day Top pattern is an intriguing prospect. It is the same form as the Bullish Engulfing that you will see in the next part of this chapter, but the difference is that it comes in an uptrend and its meaning is the opposite; that is, it presages a change to a market downturn. For effectiveness, you should look for the preceding uptrend to be long established, and thus, getting tired.

For the reversal signal to be considered valid, you need to check what the closing price is on the following day. If it is below the white candle close, then the pattern and the reversal are considered confirmed.

Tweezer Top

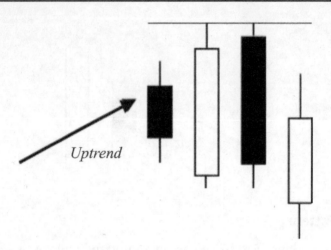

Uptrend

General Pattern

The Tweezer Top is better explained as a concept, rather than as a specific pattern. It consists of two candlesticks that have a high at the same level. The high may be the upper shadow, the opening, or the closing price, just as long as it is the greatest price for the day. This means that the candlesticks can be either color, so the above is just one of many possible examples.

Meaning

This is not a very significant pattern, but it can have added importance if the tweezer candles form or are part of another candlestick reversal signal, such as a Harami. Its meaning comes from the established idea of support and resistance levels on a price graph. In this case, the fact that two candles have reached up to a certain level, but not exceeded it, implies that the level may be a resistance to a further price increase.

This view would be reinforced if there has been a long run up to the level, meaning that the rally may be running out of steam; or if the level has been previously reached and not exceeded; or if a third candlestick also reaches up to touch the level without breaking through it. If the price will not go higher, the inference is that the price will reverse and fall back.

Bullish Engulfing

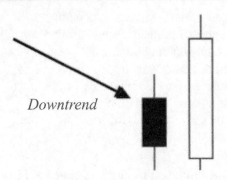

Downtrend

General Pattern

The Bullish Engulfing pattern is a common one and is similar to the Bearish Engulfing. The second candlestick is larger than the first, and the pattern is more powerful the larger it is. The volume on the first day is usually low, indicating that the selling off of the bear market is losing steam. In contrast, the second bull day has a higher volume, which shows that the sentiment has changed.

The shadows are only significant in that short shadows on the first day strengthen the signal. What matters is that no part of the first real body is outside the second real body.

Meaning

As noted above, the first candle indicates that the downtrend has lost its power. The second candle is just the market picking up sympathy to go in a new direction. The pattern would be confirmed if the third day continued the reversal and opened higher.

The Bullish Engulfing pattern and the Piercing Line pattern, which follows, are just two of the named candlestick patterns that Dr. Barry Burns mentions in his case study.

CASE STUDY: DR. BARRY BURNS

Dr. Barry Burns is a businessman who has owned several small companies. His business background had taught him to focus on the bottom line, so his study of the financial markets was for one purpose only: to make profits. He started his study of the markets under the direction of his father, Patrick F. Burns, who accumulated more than 70 years of trading experience before passing away in 2005.

Burns furthered his education by reading over 100 books on trading and investing, and spent over $50,000 in trading courses and education. In addition, he hired three professional traders to mentor him personally. He even flew to Chicago to work with a former floor trader at the Chicago Mercantile Exchange.

All of this research and study resulted in insights that eventually led to the development of his own methodology.

He has been the featured speaker at DayTradersUSA, and he developed a five-day course for WorldWideTraders. Burns has been a headlining guest speaker for the Market Analysts of Southern California, has given seminars around the country at many Wealth Expos and Traders Expos and has been interviewed on the Robin Dayne "Elite Masters of Trading" Radio Show.

Burns was the former lead moderator of FuturesTalk chat room, where he would guide listeners through the open and close of each trading day. He has a doctorate in hypnotherapy and is a certified NLP practitioner and is therefore able to help people with the psychology of trading. He started his own education firm, Top Dog Trading, to help students become profitable and avoid the lengthy, expensive learning curve he experienced.

Burns offers a free, five-day video trading course at **www.topdogtrading. com/free_course.html** and may be contacted at barry@topdogtrading. com.

CASE STUDY: DR. BARRY BURNS

What type of trading do you use candlesticks with — what markets and time periods?

I trade equities (mostly various indexes, but occasionally individual stocks), futures, and currencies. The time frames I use for trading range from 100-tick charts for day trading, to daily and even weekly charts for swing trading and investing. I use the same technical analysis techniques for all of my trading, regardless of market or time period.

When and how did you start getting interested in trading?

My father started trading when he was 18, so I've been around trading and the markets all my life. My dad would do research on several stocks and then sit me down at the kitchen table and present the research to me. We'd analyze it together, and he'd ask me to choose a stock. We'd then watch all of the stocks to see how they performed. That was a great learning experience. It helped teach me what mattered and what didn't, and also, I got to see the ups and downs of the markets over long periods of time. I was pretty young, about 9 or 10, when we started that exercise.

My interest in the market began then, but I didn't have a passion for it. I was more interested in football, hockey, and kung-fu!

Later in life, when I was looking for a new occupation, I conducted research to find the perfect career. I had been overworked, underpaid, and was tired of having to report to people who usually knew less than I did.

Trading rose to the top of my research because I wouldn't have a boss, I would have complete time freedom, and it had the potential for making a truckload of money. It was the perfect combination of things I was looking for.

So I started looking at it seriously again, and once I did, I was immediately passionate about it.

I called my dad and went back to Detroit to spend some time with him and be mentored by him some more.

After that, I dove into every book I could find, joined a local trading club, attended seminars and courses, and, over the years, hired three mentors to work with me on a personal level.

CASE STUDY: DR. BARRY BURNS

Did you use candlestick charts from the start of your trading? If not, how much difference do you think they made to your trades when you learned to interpret them?

I didn't use candlestick charts at the beginning of my trading. I originally learned with good, old-fashioned Western bars and traded with them for a few years. When I was introduced to candlestick charts, they looked very foreign to me since I was accustomed to Western bars. However, I also found them very intriguing, so I educated myself about them, and it wasn't long before I realized how much more information they provided at a glance. I was a pretty quick convert.

Do you enter a trade on the basis of a candlestick pattern only — always, sometimes, or never?

I always consider the candlestick pattern when I trade, but I never enter a trade based exclusively on it. My entire trading plan is designed around waiting for the various "energies" of the market to align in the same direction at the same time.

Price pattern is one of those energies. But I also look at trend, cycle, momentum, support/resistance, fractals, and volume.

Candlestick patterns are very powerful, but in my trading, they carry more significance when they occur at the right time and in the right place on the chart, so I don't trade them in an isolated manner. I only trade them in the context of what else is occurring in the chart.

What other indicators do you use in conjunction with candlesticks if you want confirmation? Which do you find work best in combination with candle signals?

I look for candlestick patterns in combination with moving averages, the stochastic indicator, and MACD. I also look for the candlesticks to occur at support/resistance levels. Generally, I don't make a trade without looking at the next higher time frame to see the bigger picture of what the markets are doing and where that candlestick is appearing in the bigger picture.

CASE STUDY: DR. BARRY BURNS

There are many named candlestick patterns. Do you find that you only focus on a few, and if so which?

I don't use all of the candlestick patterns. Here are the ones I use:

Bullish and Bearish Engulfing Patterns

Dark Cloud Cover

Evening Star

Hammer

Hanging Man

Morning Star

Narrow Range Doji

Piercing Pattern

Shooting Star

Spinning Top

Is this just because you find them the most effective, or is it also because of other factors, such as how often they occur, for example?

These are just the patterns that make sense to me and that I can visually identify quickly without having to think too much. When I'm day trading I have to make very quick decisions, so I only use a few patterns that really stand out to me and are immediately evident.

Piercing Line

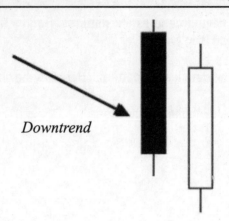

Downtrend

General Pattern

The Piercing Line occurs in a downward trending market and comprises two long days. The first is black and confirms the trend, with the price still dropping. On the second day, the market opens lower still, but heads upward to close above the midpoint of the previous day.

There are two conditions that must be complied with: The second day must open below the lowest point of the previous day (not the close), and it must go up to above the midpoint by the close. The close will be within the body of the previous day; otherwise, the pattern would be the Bullish Engulfing.

Meaning

The second day gap continues the bearish market, but this is rapidly overtaken by the rally, which suggests that the bears have lost control and the bottom has been reached. The higher the close on the second day, the more likely it is that the reversal will happen. This pattern is the bullish equivalent of the Dark Cloud Cover.

Bullish Meeting (Counterattack) Line

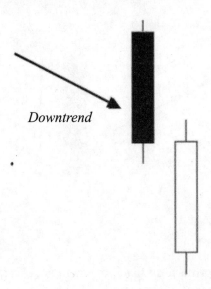

Downtrend

General Pattern

The Bullish Meeting Line pattern consists of two consecutive long days of opposite colors. It comes in a bearish downtrend, which the first long day continues. The second day gaps down, still very bearish, and then the sentiment turns around and a long bull candle follows, closing at the same price as the first day's close. This is similar to the Piercing Line, though as the close does not rise into the first day's real body, so it is not as strong.

Meaning

The turnaround in sentiment on the second day is clear and may cause traders to start buying. This can fuel the reversal in the trend. Such a move would be confirmed if the next day opened and closed higher still.

One White Soldier

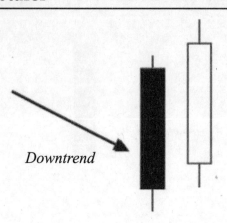

Downtrend

General Pattern

This pattern starts with a long black day, which reflects the bearish trend it is in. The second day opens higher than the previous close and closes higher than the previous open, making a long white day.

Meaning

The first candle shows that the downtrend is continuing. The second day completely reverses this sentiment, essentially breaking the bearish mood and suggesting a bullish reversal. You should look for a continuation of the move upward on the next day for confirmation of the reversal. This pattern is the bullish equivalent of the One Black Crow bearish pattern.

Bullish Kicking

General Pattern

The Bullish Kicking pattern comprises one long black candle followed by a long white candle. There should be little or no shadow on either candle, and the white candle is gapped completely above the black candle. The Bullish Kicking pattern, or Kicker, can occur in any market trend, not just in a bear market.

Meaning

This is one of the most powerful patterns, as is the Bearish Kicker. The first long black candle indicates a strong downward force on the price, especially considering the lack of shadows, indicating little dissension. When the next day opens above the first day and continues to rally, it provides sturdy evidence of a complete change of mood or perception in the market. Such a clear switch in sentiment demands attention from the candle watcher.

Often, there is an external reason for such a swing. For example, there may be news of a favorable takeover or a major prescription drug breakthrough.

Bullish Harami

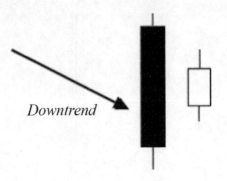

Downtrend

General Pattern

This pattern is the bullish equivalent of the Bearish Harami. Again, Harami is Japanese for pregnant, describing the pattern graphically. The first candlestick has a long black body followed by a short white candle, which is engulfed by the first. The opening price of the first is greater than the second day's close; the closing price of the first is less than the opening of the second. This pattern occurs in a downtrend.

Meaning

In an established downtrend, the first candle continues the same way. The next day opens higher, which would not be expected if the downtrend were as strong as it appeared the day before, and this may make some traders buy to cover their short positions. Of course, this action may force the price to rise.

You may even see increased volume on this day, caused partly by these traders, and note that this is different from the Bearish Harami, where you may expect reduced volume on the second day. If the third day closes higher, then the reversal of trend is confirmed.

Bullish Harami Cross

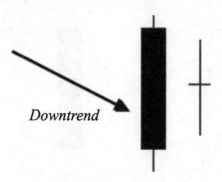

Downtrend

General Pattern

The Bullish Harami Cross is a long black body on the first day, followed by a doji on the second, which falls within the range of the first body. It is similar to the Bullish Harami.

Meaning

As with the bearish counterpart, the change of the short candle in the general Harami to a doji adds more significance to the pattern. Unless there are many doji in the price chart, you need to pay attention whenever a doji occurs, as it exemplifies indecision and doubt with no strong trend prevailing. Add to this the message of the Harami, which reveals uncertainty in the market, and you have a pattern that needs to be watched.

Bullish Doji Star

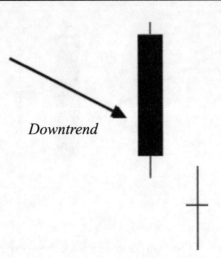

Downtrend

General Pattern

The Bullish Doji Star is a long day in the direction of the prevailing downtrend, followed by a gap downward to the next day's open. The second day has a small amount of price movement and finishes up at the same price as the open, forming a doji.

Meaning

The doji is a powerful indication that there is uncertainty in the market, and the momentum has been lost. The Bullish Doji Star shows that the downtrend is supported strongly in the first day of the pattern. However, the second day crushes any confidence that traders may have been feeling by denying the trend, even after a gap downward for the opening, with a close at or near the open. The reversal would be confirmed by a higher opening on the following day.

Homing Pigeon

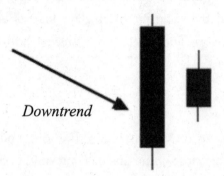

Downtrend

General Pattern

As you can see, the Homing Pigeon is very similar to the Harami. The difference is that the two candles are both the same color. Occurring in a downtrend, the Homing Pigeon consists of a long black body followed by a short black body, which is totally contained within the previous long body.

Meaning

This is the bullish equivalent of the bearish Descending Hawk. The downtrend is continued with the long black body on the first day. The opening price is up on the next day but goes down slightly during trading. It shows a general failing of the downtrend, although it is only a weak signal of reversal.

Matching Low

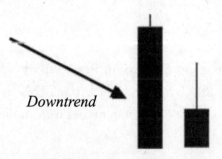

Downtrend

General Pattern

The Matching Low pattern is similar to the Homing Pigeon, with a long black day followed by a shorter black day. The difference is that both days have the same closing price and a shaved bottom. It comes in a downtrend.

Meaning

The first day confirms the downtrend with a long body. The second day opens higher than the close of the first day, but sinks back down to it by the close. You might think that this was a sign of the bearish trend continuing, but it has a different interpretation. As the closing value is identical for both days, the pattern tends to imply that this level is the bottom of the current downtrend. The level has been confirmed by having two candles going down to it, but no lower, and this is a classic example of an indication of support, which would be reinforced if any future candles stopped at the same level.

Last Engulfing Bottom

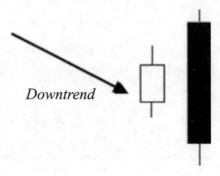

Downtrend

General Pattern

The Last Engulfing Bottom comprises a short white-bodied candle followed and engulfed by a long black one. This pattern occurs in an established downtrend, which differentiates it from the Bearish Engulfing pattern.

Meaning

This pattern is a bullish pattern, despite having the appearance of the Bearish Engulfing pattern. To be confirmed as a reversal, it is generally acknowledged that it should be followed by a candle that closes above the black candle opening. This pattern would typically be found after the downtrend has been in place for some time, and the reversal springs from a tiredness in the trend and a change in sentiment.

Tweezer Bottom

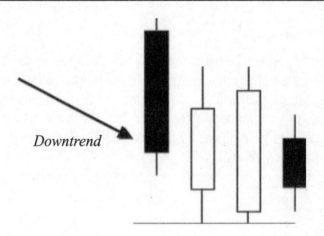

Downtrend

General Pattern

Coming in a downtrend, the Tweezer Bottom occurs when two candles achieve the same lowest price. The name derives from the idea of tweezers having two matching points side by side. It does not matter what color the candles are or how long any shadows are.

Meaning

As with the Tweezer Top, this pattern depends on the idea that two or more candles that stop at the same level may be indicating a support level. This may be reinforced by previous evidence of support at this price, or by a third candle stopping at this level. It may also be a previous resistance level from a time when the price was lower, as these often become the new support when breached.

● SAFETY ZONE ●

At this time, you may be wondering whether you can possibly learn to apply all the different patterns that are being introduced. The good news is that you do not need to have them memorized, as you will pick them up during the course of trading.

As you read the descriptions and meanings, take note of the reasons for the interpretations. Most of them are predictable and come from a general knowledge of how the candles are drawn — a knowledge that you now have. Occasionally, the interpretation may not be what you initially expect, and those patterns are worth further study to make sure that you can see why that is.

The two-day reversal patterns are probably the most applied, and as you look at the patterns involving more candlesticks, you will recognize how they are frequently just a development from the smaller patterns, perhaps with a confirmation candle added. There are only a limited number of forms, and you will quickly become familiar with the common ones as you study charts.

8 Candlestick Patterns — Three-Day Reversal Signals

Y ou will likely recognize many of the patterns being used in the three-day reversal signals. Some of them are as fundamental as a two-day reversal signal, as explained earlier, with a third candle showing confirmation. However, they are recognized patterns in their own right and part of the candlestick charting knowledge that you will acquire. As in the previous chapter, they are arranged with bearish reversals first, with each pattern being a development from the previous one so that you can follow the progression of the meanings.

Evening Star

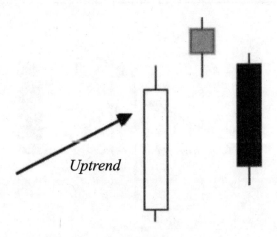

Uptrend

General Pattern

The Evening Star consists of a long white day, following the uptrend in place. The second day has a gap to the open and a small body of either color. This candle is the Star of the name. Star patterns require a gap. The third day gaps down and loses value to close within the first white real body.

There are some different views on the details of the pattern form. Some experts insist on the gap between the second and third, and some do not — the gap from first to second is important, however. Experts can also require that the third day close more than halfway into the first day's real body.

Meaning

Although it opens with a gap, the small real body of the second candle is the beginning of indecision and losing the momentum of the uptrend. When the third day gaps down, and continues down to the close, this provides more evidence that the market emotion has reversed to a bearish trend. Sometimes, a gap does not mean that the market forces are strong, but signifies the last attempt to push the market, which is shown to fail by a short body, and possibly subsequent candles, proving the reversal.

Evening Doji Star

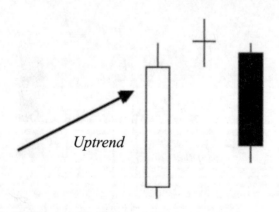

Uptrend

General Pattern

This candlestick pattern is a more specific, stronger version of the Evening Star. It comprises a long white candle, which is consistent with the uptrend. The Doji Star follows — this is a doji, as the open and close are the same, and the term Star is used because there is a gap in price between the first real body and the price of the doji. The third day gaps down and is a long black candle, giving up much of the previous gains.

Meaning

The Bearish Doji Star starts this pattern, which already suggests that a reversal may be in the cards. As explained in the chapter introduction, many three-candle patterns are simply developments from two-candle patterns. The doji is a strong indicator of uncertainty, which means that this pattern is considered a better one than the three-candle Evening Star. The third candle serves to give the confirmation the Doji Star needs, and the end result is that this is considered a significant pattern. It helps if the third black body penetrates well down into the first candle's body.

Bearish Abandoned Baby

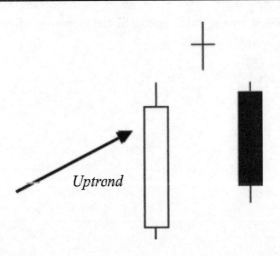

Uptrend

General Pattern

The first candle in the Bearish Abandoned Baby is a long white body, which is indicative of the existing uptrend. The second is a doji whose shadow gaps above the shadow of the first, and the third reverses the trend with a long black real body below the doji with the shadows gapped down. The long black body finishes well into the first candle's real body. This is a particular case of the Evening Doji Star and is quite rare.

The special feature that makes it an Abandoned Baby is the doji having a gap from both the preceding and following candlesticks, and this gap applies to the shadows of the candles, not just the real bodies, as commonly defined.

Meaning

The first candle continues the existing trend and serves only as a starting point for the pattern. The dramatic feature is a complete gap to a doji. The gap would suggest a strong sentiment with the trend, but this is totally nullified by the subsequent close at the open, which shows that the move may be the last gasp of a dying trend. The third candle in reverse, again with a full gap including shadows, shows that the market is quite interested in the price going in the opposite direction from the original trend.

Two Crows

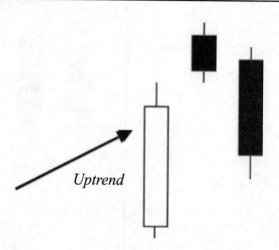

Uptrend

General Pattern

The Two Crows pattern comes in an uptrend, and the first white long candle continues that trend. The next day gaps up much higher but does reverse to close lower, although still higher than the first day's real body. The third day opens in the body of the second day and drops to close in the body of the first day. Compare this to the Evening Star, which recommends a gap between the second and third candles and requires that the third candle retraces more than 50 percent into the first candle's real body.

Meaning

After a long uptrend, the gap up is followed by some sign of weakness in the fall to the close on the second day. The third day's open tries again to rally the price, but the selloff shows that the bulls are losing the fight to maintain control. If this bearishness continues into the next day, it would serve as further evidence of a bearish reversal.

Upside Gap Two Crows

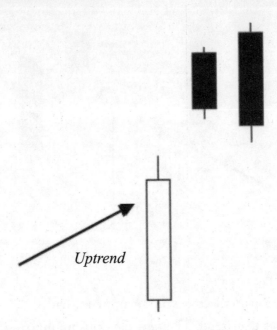

Uptrend

General Pattern

Occurring in an uptrend, the Upside Gap Two Crows is very rare. It starts with a long white candlestick that is keeping with the trend. It is followed by a gap up to the two black candlesticks, or Two Crows, giving it its name.

The two black candlesticks are both gapped up from the first candlestick, and the last engulfs the other black candlestick. The close of the last candlestick is still above the close of the first.

Meaning

The first candlestick is keeping with the uptrend and indicates a continuing trend. As the second day starts higher, the fact that it closes as a bearish candle is the first sign of trouble in the trend, but as it is still above the first candle's close, it is not seen as a large issue. However, when the third day starts higher still, and the rally cannot be maintained, finishing lower than the second day, this move has to worry the bulls, who are failing to find traction. While the third candlestick is at a higher range than with the Two Crows pattern, the size of the third bearish candle carries evidence that the bulls have no control anymore.

Bearish Tri Star

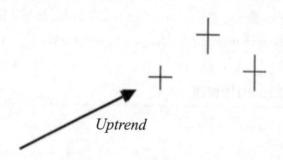

Uptrend

General Pattern

A very unusual pattern, the Bearish Tri Star comprises three consecutive doji candlesticks. The second candlestick gaps up from the first, including a gap in the shadows. This is the Star configuration. The third doji is below the second, and if there is a gap between the second and third, this strengthens the pattern's meaning.

Meaning

This pattern is the last in the series of three-candle reversal patterns gapping up between the first and second candles, which began with the Evening Star. If you see it, your first action should be to determine whether it is a valid pattern, as it is quite rare. You can look at the volume of trading on each day and make sure that it represents an active market and that there are no data errors.

The Tri Star is likely to occur after a long trend, when the momentum weakens and the candles generally get shorter. The first doji is a sign of uncertainty in itself and would draw your attention to this stock. The second doji, with a jump in price that is enough to gap even the shadows, is a desperate attempt to continue the trend. This attempt is shown as lacking any force by the fact that the trading does not move the price, and the close comes at the opening price to make a second doji.

When the price drops to form a third doji, it serves to emphasize the overwhelming indecision in the market at this time. It will be enough for many traders to give up their holdings, causing a reversal in trend.

Three Outside Down

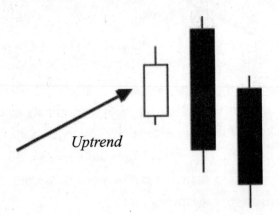

Uptrend

General Pattern

The Three Outside Down pattern is a Bearish Engulfing pattern with a confirming bearish candlestick on the following day. The form is a small white body on the first day; a second day that opens higher and closes lower than the body on the first day, giving the engulfing pattern; and finally, a black candlestick on the third day that closes lower.

Meaning

You may recognize from the first two candlesticks, that a reversal is being indicated. The first candlestick may be based on light volume and generally shows that the bull trend is slowing. The open above and then close below on the second day sets the scene for a bearish takeover of control. When the third day is a black candlestick, with a steady price decline indicated during the day, you can consider that the Engulfing pattern is confirmed by the market, and a reversal is underway.

Three Inside Down

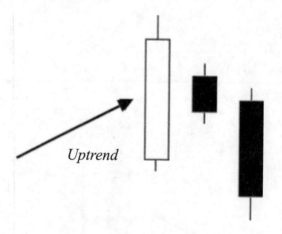

Uptrend

General Pattern

The Three Inside Down is not a classic, Japanese candlestick pattern but an addition that has been found useful in Western trading. It is simply the two-candle, Harami pattern, a very common chart pattern, augmented with a third candle confirming the reversal. The bearish Harami is a long white candle in an uptrend, followed by a short black reversal candle whose real body is totally within the real body of the first candle.

The third candle is a bearish black candle that finishes lower and can be used for confirmation of the reversal.

Meaning

The psychology of this pattern is similar to the Harami. The first candle is in the trend, and the second shows a reversal of the mood. The second candle will often be based on a lower volume of trading, showing that the bull run is getting tired.

The third candle is in the direction of the reversal and is said to confirm it. The close on the third day is lower, indicating that the bears are in control now.

Three Black Crows

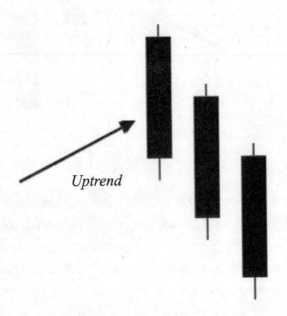

Uptrend

General Pattern

The Three Black Crows pattern occurs in an uptrend and comprises three long black candles stepping downward. The shadows are not long, and each day starts about halfway down the body of the previous day.

Meaning

With three long black days in succession getting progressively lower, the reversal of the uptrend is being clearly spelled out by the market. This pattern often occurs after a long uptrend and maybe at an established high. The first long black day sets the tone that the market has been waiting for, and the second and third days show that the traders have gotten over their bullish mentality and are selling off.

Interestingly, at **HotCandlestick.com,** they have found another use for the Three Black Crows pattern, which they talk about in this case study.

CASE STUDY: HOTCANDLESTICK.COM

HotCandlestick

admin@hotcandlestick.com

HotCandlestick.com, LLC

www.hotcandlestick.com

What type of trading do you use candlesticks with — what markets and time periods?

I'm a swing trader. I use daily and weekly candlesticks as part of my decision making process. I do not use hour or minute charts. As a starting point, for screening purposes, I filter stocks within the S&P 500. I rely on fundamentals such as a strong cash position, sector, and growth potential for the next two years. Before trading, I find a stock based on my fundamental analysis, then turn to the stock chart searching for what look to me like the best technicals.

CASE STUDY: HOTCANDLESTICK.COM

When and how did you start getting interested in trading?

I traded my first stock in the summer of 1987, so 2008 was the third stock market crash I have survived. I have always enjoyed the challenge of creating wealth in the face of what I felt was better odds than Las Vegas and the lottery. Statistical analysis of stock price and volume is very interesting to me.

Did you use candlestick charts from the start of your trading? If not, how much difference do you think they made to your trades when you learned to interpret them?

No. I primarily relied on loose fundamental analysis and PEG. In my early trading days, I followed company news, earnings, and a few other fundamentals closely to determine my positions. Learning candlesticks was only one of many technical analysis tools I added to my toolkit. I believe that candlesticks have helped me to significantly improve my performance; however, I cannot give you a percent contribution to my improvement, since I did not break down each technical indicator into discrete contribution amounts. It's Nov. 19, 2008 as I answer this question. The whole market has been hammered lately, and I, just as most traders, have not done well this year. I do not short stocks; however, I have kept a cash position ready to pick up these incredible bargains very soon.

Do you enter a trade on the basis of a candlestick pattern only — always, sometimes, or never?

Never. I use fundamental analysis and several other technical indicators in conjunction with candlesticks.

What other indicators do you use in conjunction with candlesticks if you want confirmation? Which do you find work best in combination with candle signals?

Stochastics, RSI, IMI, and MACD are technical indicators I routinely follow, along with candlesticks. I also watch the stock price relative to the 20,2 Bollinger Bands. A confirmation I like to use is the crossover of the fast stochastic & HCS IMI, which is found on the stock charts at **HotCandlestick.com**.

CASE STUDY: HOTCANDLESTICK.COM

Do you find filters, such as price or volume, effective in assisting selection of worthwhile candlestick patterns?

Yes. If there is large volume at a price level (volume by price on the chart) that certain candlestick patterns are close to, then I may assign it extra weighting in my selection criteria.

There are many named candlestick patterns. Do you find that you only focus on a few, and if so, which?

One of several candlestick patterns I follow as a value swing trader is the Bearish Three Black Crows pattern. If that pattern is found at the bottom of a recent sharp decline (negative strength), then I'm inclined to buy. Since it's a reversal pattern, it should be found at the top of a recent up move in stock price. However, at **HotCandlestick.com**, we track most patterns no matter what price trend they are found in and then assign a strength value. If the strength is positive, then the candlestick pattern is found in the expected price trend.

Is this just because you find them the most effective, or is it also because of other factors, such as how often they occur, for example?

In the case of the Three Black Crows candlestick pattern, it helps me to identify extreme oversold stocks. Since I'm a value swing trader, I prefer to buy low and sell high (versus buying high and selling higher). The site, **HotCandlestick.com**, tracks 66 candlestick patterns and tracks the frequency and historical performance of each candlestick pattern by stock ticker symbol. Subscribers have access to the extensive searching and sorting capabilities of the HotCandlestick databases.

Identical Three Crows

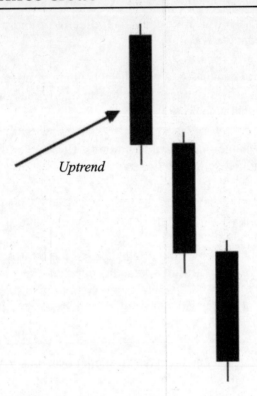

Uptrend

General Pattern

This is a special case of the Three Black Crows and comprises three long black days after an uptrend. Compared to the Three Black Crows, these are spaced down more, with each day's candle opening at around the closing price of the previous day. The shadows are short and insignificant.

Meaning

This is an even more bearish reversal of the trend than the Three Black Crows. The psychology shows selling that is almost in panic mode, with hardly any buying strength at all. A strong bear market is indicated.

Unique Three Mountain Top

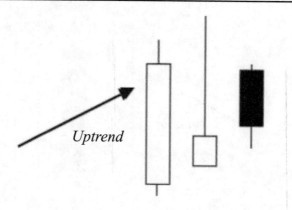

Uptrend

General Pattern

The Unique Three Mountain Top is a candlestick pattern that you will seldom see. It comes in an uptrend, and the first candle is a long white day, which is a continuation of that trend.

The second day opens lower and rallies to above the first day's upper shadow, but falls back to make a short white body. The third day opens higher, although not higher than the high of the second day, and falls to close above the second day's close.

Meaning

The first candle shows the trend that is in place. The second day suggests some bearish sentiment by opening lower, but the bulls try hard, setting the new high. The strength of the bulls is tested by a decline that establishes a closing price only a little above the open. The bearish sentiment seems to be overpowering the bulls.

The third day shows some stability coming to the market but in a bearish direction. If the next day is also downward, then that confirms the change in trend.

Bearish Stick Sandwich

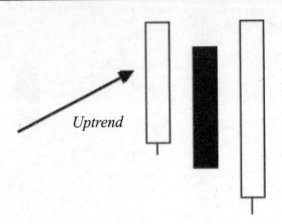

Uptrend

General Pattern

The Stick Sandwich pattern is so named because a candle is "sandwiched" between two candles of the opposite color. The Bearish Stick Sandwich comes in an uptrend, and the first candlestick is white bodied, in keeping with the trend. The second candle is a black bearish day that opens below the first day's close and closes below the first day's open. The third day opens lower still, but rallies during the day to close at the same level as the first day. The shadows are not very significant.

Meaning

You may recognize a version of the Last Engulfing Day Top in the last two candles. These candles can also represent a Bullish Engulfing pattern, but you will note that the trend is the wrong way for this. The pattern is set for a reversal to take place, but the wise course would be to find confirmation in other indicators or by watching the next day's trading.

You may also see that the tops of the first and third candles, being at the same level, may be hitting a resistance area that would add force to the implication that there will be a consolidation in the price. This can be checked against the historical levels to see whether this level has been reached but not broken before.

Bearish Squeeze Alert

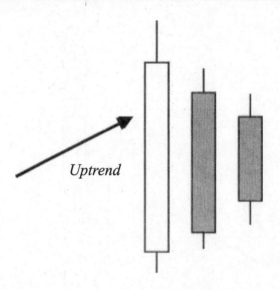

Uptrend

General Pattern

The Bearish Squeeze Alert comes in an uptrending market and consists of an initial long white-bodied candle, followed by two candles of either color, which are progressively smaller. That is, each successive candle has a lower body top and a higher body bottom than the previous one.

Meaning

If you have followed any charting techniques, you may recognize the idea of this pattern. In conventional analysis, a price that becomes limited to an increasingly narrower range, compressing into a triangle, is an important indicator. The price will break out of the restrictions of the triangle, in either direction, and start a new trend.

The direction of breakout is not certain, but the current market is stalling, so on balance, you may expect the trend to reverse. The pattern indicates a need to watch the stock closely for a sign of a breakout, and as with many potential reversal patterns, it is useful to wait and see which way the price will go before trading or look for other confirming factors.

Advance Block

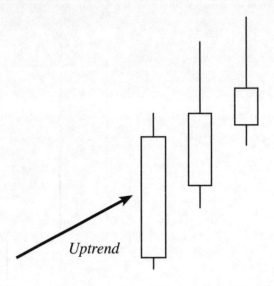

Uptrend

General Pattern

Occurring in an uptrend, the Advance Block pattern commences with a typical long white candle consistent with the trend. The following two days, the candles are white but are reducing in length and strength. Look for evidence that the bulls are trying to push the price up, as the upper wicks are long. When the price cannot be sustained at the close of each day, this shows that the bulls are failing, indicating a potential reversal.

Meaning

This pattern shows a failing in the bullish trend. The bulls are clearly having a tussle and not finding traction for the increasing prices that they keep attempting to establish, and this shows their weakness. A confirmation of the reversal would be advised before taking action on this pattern.

Bearish Deliberation

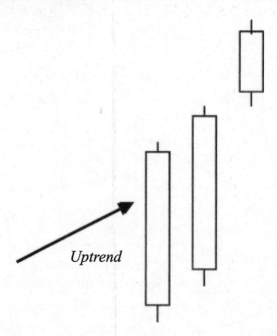

Uptrend

General Pattern

The Bearish Deliberation reversal pattern comes in an uptrend and is similar in some ways to the Advance Block. There are two long white bodies followed by a shorter white candlestick, which gaps up from the second day.

Meaning

The first two candlesticks are fully engaged with the prevalent trend, but the third candle, although still in the same direction, shows some indecision in that it has a smaller real body. You can compare it to the Evening Star pattern, which is also a bearish reversal.

The weakness of the bulls is not as evident at the start of this pattern as it is with the Advance Block, which has a progressive weakness growing through the days. For the Deliberation pattern, the weakness happens all on the last day. Some other confirmation should be sought if you intend to trade on this pattern.

Three Stars in the North

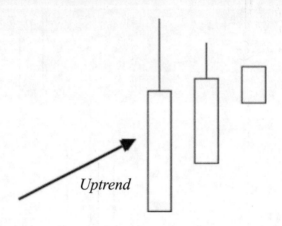

Uptrend

General Pattern

The Three Stars in the North pattern is a three-candle, bearish reversal pattern. Note the long upper shadow on the first candlestick that starts the pattern and that each successive day makes a higher close and a lower high, narrowing the range. Compare this pattern with the two previous similar patterns.

Meaning

The long upper shadow presages the expected market turnaround of this pattern. In effect, it is the bulls testing a high and not having the strength to maintain it through to the day's close. This starts the evident deterioration in the uptrend.

The weakening of the trend is shown in the second day, with a reduced range, and again, a very evident upper shadow, which shows the bulls failing, with selling down to the close. The third day should have no shadows, although small shadows are acceptable. This pattern is quite rare, and strict adherence to the guidelines will probably not be possible.

Morning Star

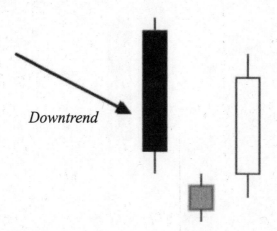

Downtrend

General Pattern

The opposite of the Evening Star, the Morning Star occurs in a downtrend, and it is the first of the downward trending, three-candle reversal patterns we shall look at. The first candle is in keeping with the trend, being a long black body. The second day gaps down at the open, but comprises a short body, giving the Star configuration of the pattern name. The third candle shows a reversal of the trend, with a gap up, and a real body that rises into the real body of the first candlestick.

Some authorities do not demand a gap between the second and third candles to establish this pattern.

Meaning

The first candle line confirms the current downward trend. The gap is bearish, but the short body shows some doubt entering the psychology of the market. The following day, the gap upward and the long bullish body show that a reversal is underway.

Morning Doji Star

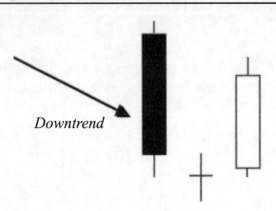

Downtrend

General Pattern

The Doji Star was introduced in the previous two-day pattern section and comprises in this bullish version a long black candle in a downtrend followed by a doji gapped down from the real body. The gap qualifies this to be called a Star. What makes this into a Morning Doji Star is the third white candlestick, which gaps up from the doji and closes well into the real body of the first candlestick, providing the confirmation that the Doji Star needs.

Meaning

The doji is always a sign that the sentiment of the market may be changing, as it shows indecision on the part of the traders. This pattern surrounds the doji with evidence of this change in sentiment, from the initial candle, which continues the preceding trend, through the change indication of the doji, to a long candle in the opposite direction. This Morning Doji Star pattern represents a more powerful version of the Morning Star because of the power of the doji to represent indecision.

Bullish Abandoned Baby

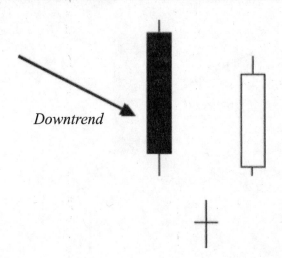

Downtrend

General Pattern

As with the bearish version of the Abandoned Baby, the "baby" is the doji in the middle that is gapped from both the preceding and following candles. The first candle is a long black candle, which is in the downtrend. The second is the doji, and note that the shadows, not just the bodies, of the first and second days are gapped — the "baby" is completely "abandoned." Continuing this theme, the third white candlestick is gapped up above the shadows of the doji.

Meaning

The first candle, as with many of these patterns, follows the trend and serves to set the scene. This is followed by a dramatic gap to the next day, which you might think enforces the bearish market sentiment. As the second day resolves to a doji by the close, this actually reveals the gap down to be a last attempt to maintain control by the bears, and the bullish third candle confirms that the trend has been broken.

This pattern may also be compared to the Morning Star and Morning Doji Star, which are very similar and have the same interpretation.

Two Rabbits

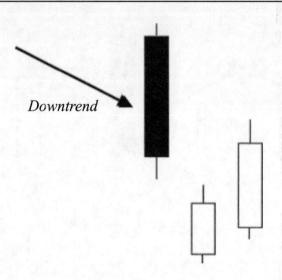

Downtrend

General Pattern

The Two Rabbits reversal pattern is bullish in a bearish downtrend. The pattern starts with a large black candle in the trend. It is followed on the second day by a gap to open lower, which is bearish, but the day rallies and closes higher, although not as high as the close of the first day. The third day opens within the body of the second and rallies far enough to close in the first day's real body.

Meaning

The first day is in keeping with the trend, but the new low on the second day is too much, and it cannot be sustained by the bears. The day closes higher, but this is not too much of a blow to the bears, as the close is still below the previous day's. On the third day, there are clearer reversal signs, especially as the gap is covered by this candle.

Downside Gap Two Rabbits

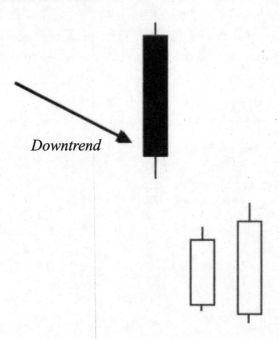

Downtrend

General Pattern

In an established downtrend, the first candle of this pattern is a long black body, concurring with the trend. The downside gap of the pattern's name is from this first candle to the two following, which are called the two rabbits. This name is given to them as they are two white, bullish candles, which are regarded as ready to jump up out of their burrow.

The third candlestick shows that the opening price was lower still, but the close was higher than the second day, although not as high as the first real body. The third candle engulfs the second.

Meaning

The first candle goes along with the established trend, as with the majority of reversal patterns. When the second day opens lower, that is also part of the trend, but the close, being higher, is not in keeping. The bears are not deterred, as the close is still below the first day's close. Taking heart from the third day opening even lower, they are then surprised by the price going up to a higher high, which implies that the market has reversed. You should look for a confirming signal or for the next day's candle, before relying on this, as the market is showing some confusion. Confusion often implies a reversal, but it may just become consolidation before continuing a trend.

Bullish Tri Star

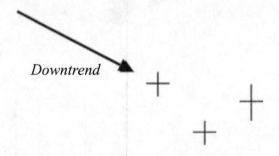

Downtrend

General Pattern

As with the Bearish Tri Star, this is a very unusual pattern, and you should check that it has been based on valid data and volume. The first candlestick is a doji, already implying uncertainty in the market. The second doji is gapped down to form a Star pattern, and this gap includes the candles' shadows. The third candle, another doji, is up from the second, and may also be gapped, which would add significance to the pattern.

Meaning

As with the bearish counterpart, this pattern is most likely to occur after a long trend, when the market is getting tired and momentum of the trend is waning. Each doji carries its own message. The first says to watch out for indecision that may bring changes. The second is a determined bearish effort, by starting out at a gap, that lacks any substance by the close at the same level. The third doji still exhibits the general confusion in the market and provides a warning to traders that the market is still uncertain. After such a combination, it is likely that any traders who have short positions would be rushing to cover them, which would support the trend reversal.

Three Outside Up

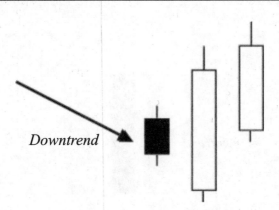

Downtrend

General Pattern

The Three Outside Up is a pattern that has been developed for the Western trader and is not a classic Japanese pattern. It is simply a Bullish Engulfing pattern on which the third day has been added, giving a confirmation of the reversal.

The Bullish Engulfing pattern is a black candle that continues the downtrend, but it may have a low volume, showing that the bears are losing momentum. This is followed by a day that starts even lower, but then rallies to finish higher, the real body of the second day engulfing the real body of the first.

The Three Outside Up pattern includes a third bullish candle, which tends to confirm the reversal and closes at a higher level.

Meaning

This pattern includes the confirming third candle, which means that the Bullish Engulfing pattern is validated. It signals a reversal of the bear trend to a bullish rallying market.

Three Inside Up

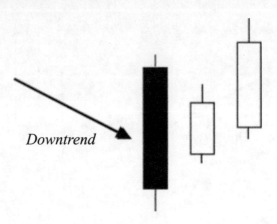

Downtrend

General Pattern

The Three Inside Up, as with many multi-candle patterns, is a development from a simpler pattern. In this case, the pattern is a Bullish Harami followed by a long white day, which is the confirmation that the Harami requires to "prove" the bullish reversal.

The first two days are a Harami, a long black day in a downtrend followed by a shorter white candlestick, which is wholly within the real body of the first day. The third day is a white bullish candle that closes higher.

Meaning

This pattern has the same meaning as the Harami. The long black day is in trend, but the second day starts low and rallies against the trend. The rally is not strong, and there may be small volume on that day.

On the third day, the bulls come out and make it a longer candlestick in their direction. This tends to confirm that the reversal from bearish to bullish is genuine.

Three White Soldiers

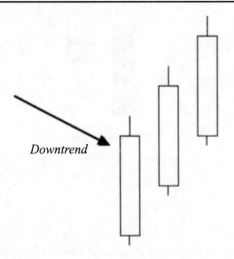

Downtrend

General Pattern

This is a pattern that is an important part of Sakata's Method, one of the original analysis tools used in Japan, which is discussed later. It is simply three long white candles in succession, each starting about halfway up the previous real body. The shadows are small.

Meaning

This occurs in a downtrend and is thus a strong reversal signal. It represents a consistent bullish tendency. Each day opens lower than the previous close, which shows that even with a strong bull move, there will almost always be some selling, but each day sets new highs, confirming the trend reversal.

Unique Three River Bottom

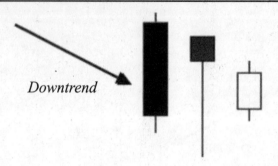

Downtrend

General Pattern

This is an extremely unusual pattern, starting with a long black day in a downtrend. The second day opens higher and trades down below the first day, but then closes back up near the open, producing only a small body. The lower shadow is at least three times as long as the body.

On the third day, the open is lower, but not as low as the extreme low of the second day. The third day is bullish, with a white body that still closes below the second day's close.

Meaning

This particular set of candlesticks is rare. You can see a Hammer in the second day, which would tend to support the reversal signal. Although the second day opens higher than the first closed, the pressure from the bears pushes a new low, but this cannot be sustained, which calls into question who is controlling the market. Despite the close being forced up, the third day is back down again at the open. More indecision is shown, which is further confused by this turning into a bullish day but one that could not finish as high as the second day at the close.

As the market seems very confused, you should look for a higher candle on the next day to confirm the reversal.

Bullish Stick Sandwich

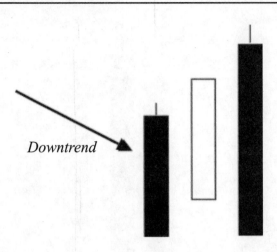

Downtrend

General Pattern

As with its counterpart from the bearish section of this chapter, the Bullish Stick Sandwich gets its name from the sandwiching of one color between two candles of the other color. In this case, it starts with a black body in a downtrend. The second day is a white body that starts higher and goes higher still. The third day, the opening price is up further but drops to close at the same level as the first day's close.

Meaning

This pattern is not straightforward to interpret, as it is a mixture of signals. Note the Bearish Engulfing form in the last two candles. That pattern is applicable in an uptrending market, though, and the meaning in this case is usually the opposite, reversing to a rally. One reason for this is the two candles closing at the same level, which may indicate a support position. You can look at previous price movements to see whether this level has been a support before.

You should seek some sort of confirmation with other indications to improve the performance of this trade.

Bullish Squeeze Alert

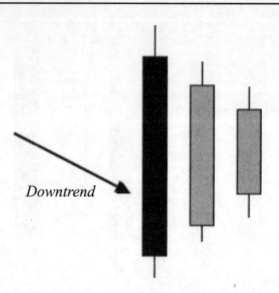

Downtrend

General Pattern

As was mentioned in considering the Bearish Squeeze Alert, the pattern here is a triangular shape formed from three candles. This gives the "squeeze" to the price. The first candlestick is a bearish, long black candle that is in the prevailing trend, and this is followed by progressively shorter-bodied candles with lower tops and higher bottoms to their real bodies. These can be either color.

Meaning

The price is squeezed into a smaller range over the days of the pattern, and the result is that the price will break out of the pattern. The direction in which the price may break out is uncertain, but as the reduction in the range is actually a consequence of the market stalling, it would be likely to be in the reverse direction to the trend — that is, upward.

When a price breaks out, it is likely to keep going in that direction, establishing a new level.

Descent Block

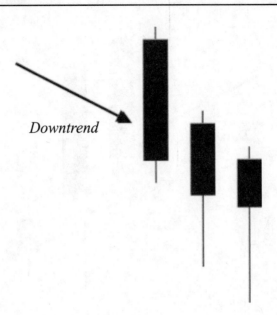

Downtrend

General Pattern

In an established downtrend, the first candle supports that trend with a long black day. The second and third days are progressively shorter, although continuing the downward move, and the long lower shadows of these two days show some bearish activity, although on each day, the closing price came back up.

Meaning

The Descent Block is similar to Three Black Crows, but the meaning is the opposite. It comes in a downtrend and signals a reversal to that trend. The bears try on the second and third days to establish lower prices, but the prices do not stick into the close of the days. While at first glance, the pattern seems to agree with the downtrend, on closer examination, the long lower shadows show that the bears' grip on the market is weakening.

Bullish Deliberation

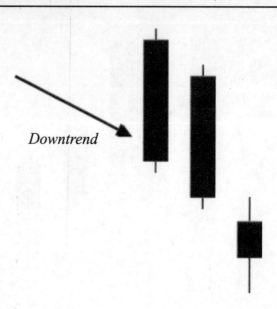

Downtrend

General Pattern

The Bullish Deliberation pattern is similar to the Descent Block, discussed previously. In a downward market, the first two long black candles continue in the trend. The third candlestick is a shorter black candlestick, and it gaps below the other two.

Meaning

While the first two candles would seem to support a continued decline in price, the short body of the third candle and the gap down call the strength of the move into question. You could compare this to the Star pattern, where the gap down means that the market may be getting overstretched and will need to have a period of consolidation, which, in this context, means a rally in prices.

Three Stars in the South

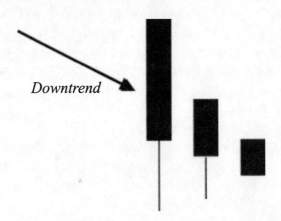

Downtrend

General Pattern

In a downtrend, the Three Stars in the South pattern shows a progressive lessening in bearish enthusiasm in overall terms. Note that the shadows are very significant in this pattern. The lowest points reached on each day are progressively higher. In each case, the entire length of the candle is engulfed by the previous day, until the third candlestick, which has little or no shadow.

Meaning

The downtrend is obviously lessening in intensity in this pattern. Significantly, the low on the first day is extended, and the close higher up represents some buying interest. The second day opening price is higher, and this is the highest price of the day, but it soon drops to a higher low, which rallies up to a close. This indicates to the bears that the bulls are starting to fight the downtrend.

On the third day, there is little activity, and the short body represents indecision. There is another higher low, again suggesting that the bears are losing the battle.

● SAFETY ZONE ●

The three-day reversal patterns are numerous, and you cannot expect to remember them all straight away. Going through each one is a worthwhile exercise, though, as you can develop an instinct for where the pattern shows the price to be heading. Generally speaking, three or more days is long enough to establish with more certainty the true message of the candles.

That said, the more indication you can find that a reversal is due, the more sound it is to trade on the basis of the candlestick pattern signal, and you should always take note of any other factors and indicators that you may have available to strengthen your decision.

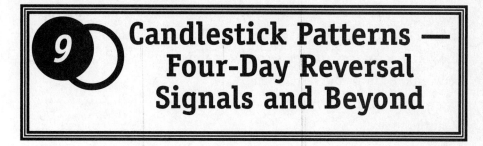

Candlestick Patterns — Four-Day Reversal Signals and Beyond

After Bottom Gap Up

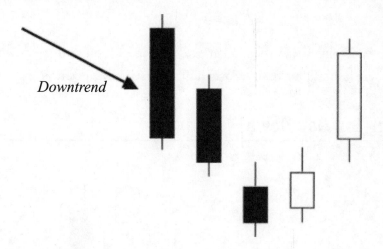

Downtrend

General Pattern

The After Bottom Gap Up pattern is rare but understanding the psychology of it allows you to analyze further patterns. The pattern occurs in an established downtrend and starts with a long black day, which is in accord with the trend. The second and third days are also black and each close lower than the previous day. The third day opens gapped down from the close of the second.

The fourth day is a long white day, and the fifth long white day opens above the close of the fourth, gapping up. That is, the pattern has two gaps: one going down between the second and third candles and one going up between the fourth and fifth candles.

Meaning

This pattern shows the progression of the market from a bearish trend to the stock becoming oversold to a bullish reversal. The first two candles are in the trend, and the third stretches the trend with a gap. The reaction to this is for the next day to be a white candle, and this change in sentiment is emphasized by the fifth day gapping up. Note that the fifth candle should still be below the starting candle and should not negate the entire move at once.

The psychology is that the market extended itself too far to the downside, and there is a bull move to recover a more sustainable position.

After Top Gap Down

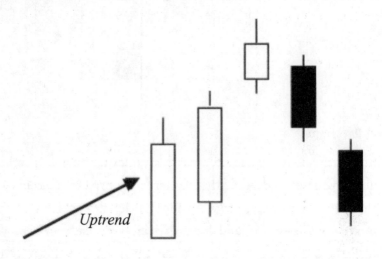

Uptrend

General Pattern

After Top Gap Down is the complimentary pattern to the After Bottom Gap Up. It is a bearish reversal pattern that starts with three white candles in the uptrend. The third candle opens higher than the previous close, gapping up, and subsequently, this is shown to have overextended the bullish move. The fourth and fifth candles are long black days, and significantly, the fifth gaps down from the close of the fourth.

Meaning

The psychology of this pattern is that the strong third-candle move is brought into question by the following black candle, showing that there is weakness developing in the rally. The fifth candle gapping down serves to reinforce this view of the market sentiment.

Bearish Breakaway

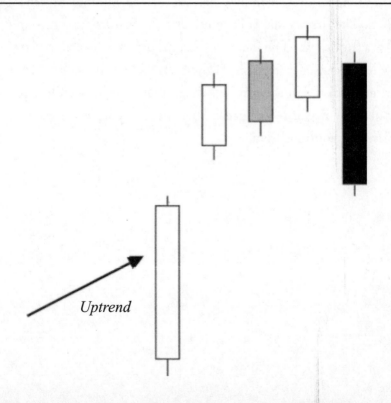

Uptrend

General Pattern

The Breakaway candlestick pattern incorporates a gap in the direction of the trend. For the Bearish Breakaway, the first candle is in the trend, a long white day, followed by a gap to a second white candlestick. The third and fourth days continue in the direction of the trend: Some say that the signal is stronger if the third day is the opposite color. The fifth day is a black long day that finishes in the gap between the first and second days.

This pattern can also be seen with only two candles, or more than three candles, between the first and the reversal candle. The only fixed requirement is that the reversal candle stretches from the previous candle back to finish in the gap.

Meaning

The meaning is quite complex because of the number of candlesticks involved. The first candle is in trend, and the gap in the direction of the trend is a strong sign. The following gradual progression serves to represent a slow down in the enthusiasm of the bulls. When the reverse candlestick occurs and finishes in the gap, it is a sign that all those candles up to that point are now negated. The gap has not been filled, so it is expected that the price will continue to fall.

Bullish Breakaway

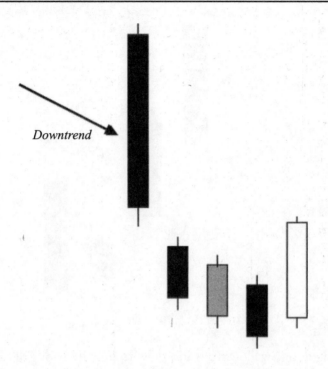

Downtrend

General Pattern

The Bullish Breakaway pattern is similar to the Bearish Breakaway in description just in the opposite direction. Again, the important part is the gap after the first candlestick in the direction of the trend. Also, the final returning candle closes in the gap, recapturing all the losses of the intermediate candles.

Meaning

The Bullish Breakaway comes in a downtrend, and is interpreted as being an acceleration by the bears, which creates an oversold condition. The gap is a strong move, which later is shown to be an overreaching move. The progression of weakening candlesticks is canceled out by the final candle taking back all the lost ground and finishing in the gap. The gap has not been filled at this point, and it is expected that it will be in subsequent days.

Concealing Baby Swallow

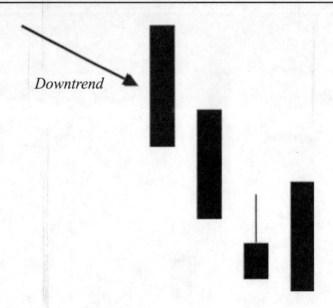

Downtrend

General Pattern

The Concealing Baby Swallow starts in a downtrend with a long black day. The second candle continues this trend. The third candlestick gaps down, trades up during the day into the body of the previous day, and finishes down again to give a short black candle. The fourth day engulfs the third, including the upper shadow.

The significant factors are the gap down to the third day and the upper shadow of the third day rising into the second day's range. Three of the candles are shown with no shadows in the figure, and this is preferred, but short shadows are acceptable.

Meaning

The first two days give strong evidence of the trend and do not show any cause to believe that the trend may change. The gapping down to the open on the third day is another exciting move for the bears. Then the price rises to above the previous close, which causes some concern, but that is fought off by the close coming back down.

All eyes are on the open of the fourth day, which gaps up from the third, starting even higher than the high shadow. This brings serious doubt to the trend, and although the market sells off to make a new low by the close, the trend is looking set to reverse. Look for other confirmation to be sure.

Ladder Bottom

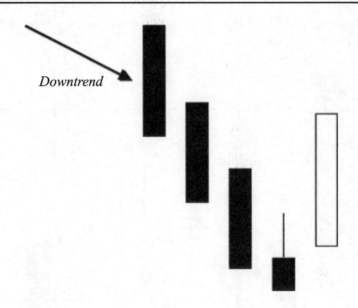

Downtrend

General Pattern

The Ladder Bottom comes in a downtrend, and starts with Three Black Crows — that is, three long black days going lower. The fourth day is also lower, but has some buying activity that pushes the price up during the day, making a long upper shadow, even though the close is down.

The fifth day opens above the last real body and does not move down, closing much higher. This may be accompanied by an increase in volume, which would strengthen the implication of the signal.

Meaning

There is an existing established downtrend, which makes the traders comfortable with their positions. The fourth day causes some pause for thought, reminding the traders that the price may not go down forever. As a result, the fifth day may see the traders who are short on the contract closing out their trades, or "buying to cover" their short position. The consequence of this is that the opening price gaps up, possibly with increased volume, and an increasing price through the day, which will make the long white body.

Ladder Top

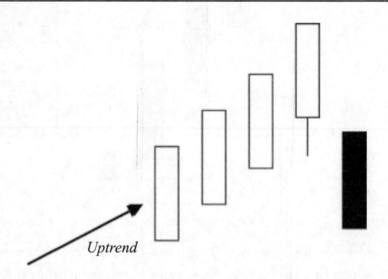

Uptrend

General Pattern

The Ladder Top pattern starts similarly to the Three White Soldiers, with three long white days progressing upward. The main difference, of course, is that the Three White Soldiers represent the bullish turn in a downtrend, and the first three candles in the Ladder Top pattern are still in trend. The fourth day is also a long white day, but it has a lower shadow that descends well into the previous day's real body, even though it closes up again.

The fifth day gaps to open below the body of the fourth day, going lower still by the close. With the exception of the fourth day's lower shadow, the other shadows, if any, are not large and do not have a bearing on the pattern.

Meaning

The start of this pattern confirms the current trend and may cause some complacency in the bullish traders. The fourth day shows some weakening in the bullish market as the price drops too low on the body of the third candle before recovering to a new high for the close. This wakes up the traders, who are long on the stock and now see that it might not go on forever.

Consequently, many traders see that it would be a good time to take their profits. This causes a reversal and a bearish candle on the fifth day.

Three Gap Downs

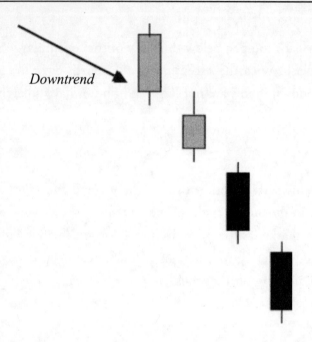

Downtrend

General Pattern

The Three Gap Downs pattern is easy to recognize. It consists of four candles in a downtrend, each of which gaps down so the real body is lower than the previous day. The last two candles should be black, and the first two can be either color.

Meaning

This is a bullish reversal pattern because the pattern is too enthusiastic in the bearish direction. The gap normally just means a strong sentiment in that direction, but the succession of three gaps may mean that the market gets oversold and is ready for a change. You should seek confirmation of the reversal because of the conflicting evidence — the strong bearish trend may remain sustained in a depressed market for a little longer.

Three Gaps Up

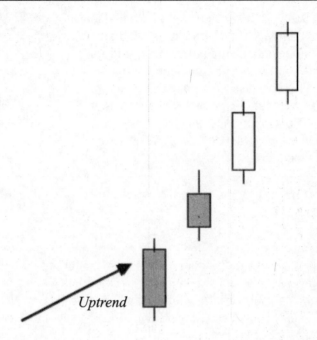

Uptrend

General Pattern

The Three Gaps Up pattern has four candlesticks and requires that each candle opens at a higher level than the previous day's close. The first two candles may be either color, and the last two are white bullish candles.

Meaning

This appears to be a strong bullish trend, and thus, you should look for confirmation of the bearish reversal. The psychology is that the market has significantly overbought this stock, and that is why the pattern may be viewed as a reversal signal. The origin of this is in Sakata's Method, which is discussed fully later. The method regards the number three as significant and suggests selling a long position after three upward gaps, as the stock may be considered overbought.

Balkrishna Sadekar, who also contributed the foreword to this book, has an extensive knowledge of candlestick charting, and tells in his case study of the patterns that he finds most relevant and engaging.

CASE STUDY: BALKRISHNA SADEKAR

Balkrishna Sadekar is the founder of Profitable Candlestick Charting, LLC. Through its Web site, **www.profitablecandlestickcharting.com**, and its various course offerings, the company educates traders in the proper use of candlestick charting. Sadekar has over ten years of U.S. stock market experience. He is currently finishing his book, *Trade Indian Stocks the Japanese Way*, to be published in India.

What type of trading do you use candlesticks with — what markets and time periods?

I personally use candlesticks for trading equities in U.S. stock markets. All Profitable Candlestick Charting courses are also based on U.S. equity markets. I also follow and recommend stocks related to Indian stock markets using candlesticks. Most of my trading is based on daily charts, what is commonly known as swing trading. Occasionally, I will look at the weekly candlestick chart.

When and how did you start getting interested in trading?

My candlestick trading journey began about six years back. I was in the 90 percent of people who bought at the top and sold at the bottom. However, a colleague of mine, who was an excellent trader, introduced me to candlestick charting. The more I studied the signals and patterns, the more it became apparent to me that the most important aspect of the stock market is not the fundamentals of the underlying companies, but the investor perception toward those companies. Candlestick charting was the best way to depict this visually.

CASE STUDY: BALKRISHNA SADEKAR

Did you use candlestick charts from the start of your trading? If not, how much difference do you think they made to your trades when you learned to interpret them?

As I mentioned, I started out in the trading world (during the 1998-99 boom and subsequent bust) with no knowledge of why stocks move. The erroneous belief that fundamentally good companies produce good stocks led to many disappointments. That, with the normal panic and greed emotions that are inherent in humans, proved to be disastrous for the portfolio. However, the use of candlestick charting and technical analysis completely reversed the results. Now, I (along with my students) am among those selling near the top and buying near the bottom. Once you know how to correctly interpret these signals and patterns, it is like having an X-ray into the market.

Do you enter a trade on the basis of a candlestick pattern only — always, sometimes, or never?

A trade is always entered on the basis of a confirmed candlestick signal. The "confirmed" part is very critical. The definition of confirmation depends on the individual stock/index chart. As an example, let us say one witnesses a Bullish Harami. The second day of the signal (bullish candle) can open and close anywhere inside the body of the first day's bearish candle. However, if the second day opens and closes in the lower half of the first day's candle, confirmation is needed the next day by a candle closing over the half-way point of the bearish candle. This is because the Japanese have defined the half-way point of tall candles as support or resistance. In the case of Bullish Harami, if the bulls cannot close the bullish candle above the half-way point of the bearish candle, then the trader needs to refrain from entering the position until the bulls prove themselves.

CASE STUDY: BALKRISHNA SADEKAR

What other indicators do you use in conjunction with candlesticks if you want confirmation? Which do you find work best in combination with candle signals?

I use stochastics to get overbought/oversold conditions for a stock or index. Candlestick signals provide high reliability in these extreme conditions. However, when stocks start trending, they might not reach these extreme conditions. In such cases, one can use the same candlestick signals at proper technical levels to enter profitable trades.

Do you use and find filters, such as price or volume, effective in assisting selection of worthwhile candlestick patterns?

Volume is a secondary conforming factor. When one witnesses a candlestick buy/sell signal in oversold/overbought conditions, and there is a volume surge, the probabilities are that much higher that the stock will reverse trend. The above-average volume shows a large amount of stock changing hands from the weak to the smart. Most investors will panic at the bottom and exuberantly buy at the top, generating the volume surge. However, no trading decision should be made based on volume alone. Candlestick signals are the primary decision-making factor.

CASE STUDY: BALKRISHNA SADEKAR

There are many named candlestick patterns. Do you find that you only focus on a few, and if so, which?

I focus on the following signals, often defined as "major candlestick signals:"

Bearish and Bullish Engulfing signal

Bearish and Bullish Harami

Dark Cloud and Piercing signal

Hanging Man and Hammer

Shooting Star and Inverted Hammer

Morning Star and Evening Star signal

Bullish and Bearish Kicker signal

Doji

Is this just because you find them the most effective, or is it also because of other factors, such as how often they occur, for example?

These major candlestick signals occur very repeatedly and with a high probability outcome, given the right technical conditions. Traders should always keep in mind that candlesticks should never be used in isolation. Proper use of technical analysis, like use of support/resistance, trend lines, and most importantly, the 50-day, simple moving average, and 200-day, simple moving average need to be applied. Trading is about putting probabilities in one's favor. The combination of candlestick signals with Western technical analysis puts the odds in the trader's favor.

● SAFETY ZONE ●

This section contains some interpretations that you may think are counterintuitive at first glance. For instance, the last pattern, Three Gaps Up, looks very strong in its forceful bullish price rises, and it may not have previously triggered your alarm mechanism as a stock that must be watched carefully for a reversal. Certainly, the pattern does not mandate a reversal, but it opens a strong possibility that the market has been too enthusiastic in the meteoric rise of the share price.

This demonstrates how the candlestick chart can provide information at a glance that you might have to look for on the Western bar chart. The gaps would not be obvious on a bar chart unless you looked closely, and it is the presence of the gaps that implies that the rally has been too forceful to be sustained.

If you see this pattern, it is easy to look for confirmation of the security being overbought by using a Western oscillator, and the pattern alerts you to check this out. While it may not be a reliable pattern on which to go short, this pattern can make you consider reducing or eliminating any long position that you currently hold, and this will protect your profits.

Candlestick Patterns — Two-Day Continuation Signals

Many traders know little about and have little to do with continuation patterns on a candlestick chart and with good reason. The most effective, profitable trading happens when you can detect and enter the market at the point of reversal or as near as possible. A continuation is in the nature of a non-event, as the stock was trending before and is trending afterward in the same way.

Nonetheless, you should become familiar with these and the psychology behind them so that you can better understand all the nuances that the candles can reveal.

Bullish Thrusting

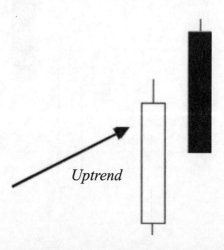

Uptrend

General Pattern

The Bullish Thrusting pattern is similar to the reversal pattern known as the Dark Cloud Cover, but it is a continuation pattern. The two-candle pattern starts with a long day in the trend, and the second day opens with a large gap in trend, which is reversed to close within the real body of the first candle. The significant points are that the gap to the second day opening price is large, and the second day close is well into the body of the first day but not more than halfway — the Dark Cloud Cover falls below halfway.

Meaning

The Bullish Thrusting pattern starts with a long white day followed by a gap up, which perpetuates the bullish view. When the day unfolds, a black bearish candle emerges, but this can be interpreted as a failure to reverse the trend because the second day falls short of the midpoint of the previous real body. If there is other confirmation that the uptrend is continuing, either by waiting for the next day or from other indicators, then this continuation pattern represents evidence of a strong bullish force as the price has been tried to the limit, and the bears failed to gain control.

Bullish In Neck Line

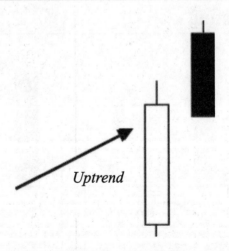

Uptrend

General Pattern

The Bullish In Neck Line pattern is similar to the previous Thrusting pattern; the difference is that the second candle does not penetrate the first candle as much. The first candlestick is a long white body in trend, and this is followed by a bullish gap up. The second day declines and closes just inside the first day's real body.

Meaning

This pattern is interpreted as the bears are attempting to take control against the trend, but are found too weak to succeed. The market has tried on a reversal attempt, and it has not worked, so the time is not right for a true reversal. Because this pattern is so close to a reversal pattern, it should be confirmed with other indications.

Bullish On Neck Line

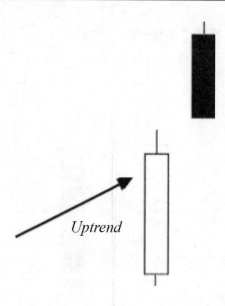

Uptrend

General Pattern

The On Neck Line is a further development in the Dark Cloud Cover, Thrusting, and In Neck Line series. The first candle is a long body in the trend. The second candle gaps to open in the trend direction but comes back to finish as the opposite color. The difference from the In Neck Line is that the return of the second candle does not make it all the way back to penetrate the first day but stops at or before the extreme price seen on day one.

Meaning

The Bullish On Neck Line occurs in an uptrend, and the first candlestick is a long white candle in trend. On the second day, the open gaps up, but the market cannot keep up the move, and the price finishes down, creating a black candle. The close is no higher than the high of the first day, which suggests that the bearish move lacks the strength to continue. If the volume is higher on the second day, this should be taken as a better indication that the uptrend will continue in due course, as it shows greater market participation by the bears, still unable to achieve a lower price.

Bullish Separating Lines

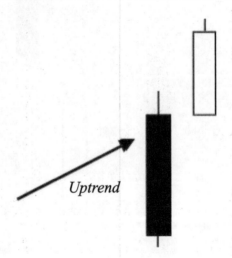

Uptrend

General Pattern

The Separating Lines are two adjacent candles of opposite color, each of which has the same opening price. The Bullish Separating Lines consist of a large black body as the first candle, which is against the trend. The second candle opens at the same price, but the price goes up, giving a white candle in trend. You can compare these with the Bullish Kicking pattern shown in the reversal section, which involves a gap up and does not need a trend for its message to be understood.

Meaning

This is a continuation pattern in that it provides some reassurance that the trend will continue after a slight pause for rest. In the case of the Separating Lines, the first candle may cause some doubt about the trend. The second candle jumps from the close of the first to open at the opening price of the first candlestick and continues in the trend direction, effectively reinstating the trend. This is an indication that the first candle was just a blip on the chart and can be ignored.

Bearish Thrusting

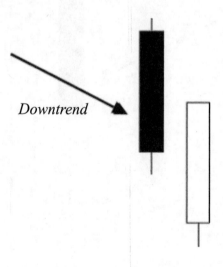

Downtrend

General Pattern

This bearish pattern is like the Piercing Line, which, you may remember, is a reversal signal. The difference is that the second candle fails to reach halfway into the body of the first candle. The first candle is a long black body, which is in the trend. The second day opens at a lower price still, gapping down and sinking lower before rallying up into the body of the previous day. The key to this being considered a continuation signal is that the rally fails to raise the price above halfway on the first day's body.

Meaning

The long black day in an uptrend is expected and in trend. The drop to a lower level on the second day opening would support the bearish view, but it is questioned by the bulls, pulling the price up to close well into the range of the first day. The close is not as high or strong as it could be, so this pattern considers that the white candle may just be a pause in the bearish decline.

Bearish In Neck Line

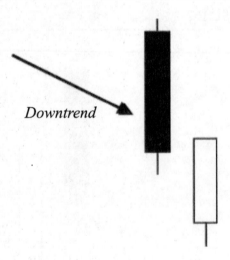

Downtrend

General pattern

The Bearish In Neck Line is similar to the Piercing Line reversal pattern and to the Bearish Thrusting continuation pattern. It comprises a large black body, which is in support of the current bearish trend followed by a white body. The second candle gaps down, reinforcing the bear move underway, but does rally up to close just inside the first candle's body.

Meaning

The significance of the Bearish In Neck Line is that the second, reversing white candlestick just touches into the previous real body, penetrating even less than the Thrusting form. The Piercing Line continues past the halfway point, which shows strength for the predicted reversal. The In Line lack of penetration indicates the weakness of the move and, by implication, that the bulls have failed to gain control, and the price will continue to fall.

Bearish On Neck Line

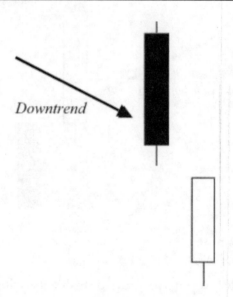

Downtrend

General Pattern

Just as with the bullish version, this is the end of a progression of patterns that started with the Piercing Line reversal. The reversal pattern has the second candle rallying up to above halfway on the first day's real body, and the subsequent Thrusting and In Neck continuation patterns close progressively lower, showing weakness. The Bearish On Neck Line pattern has the long black body of the first candlestick followed by a white body gapped down that fails to rise as far as the lowest point of the first day.

Meaning

The Bearish On Neck Line occurs in a downtrend, and the first candle supports the trend. The gap down on the second day is bearish, a sentiment that is challenged by the price rallying, but the close does not achieve the level of the previous day. The bulls attempt to take over the market is shown to have failed, and a continuation of the bearish trend can be expected.

Bearish Separating Lines

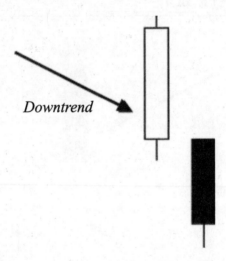

Downtrend

General Pattern

As with their bullish counterpart, the Bearish Separating Lines start with a candle in opposition to the trend — in this case, a bullish white candle. The second day opens at the same price as the first day's open and moves in the opposite direction — that is, down in price — to make a black body.

Meaning

While the first candle runs counter to the established trend, the second candle reassures that the trend is still in place and continues in the same direction. This pattern can be compared with the Bearish Kicking pattern, which is similar, but has a gap between the candles emphasizing the force of the second candle.

● SAFETY ZONE ●

You will notice that there are far fewer continuation signals than reversal signals, and as explained in the start of the chapter, this is because traders are more concerned about reversals for profitable trading. However, some of these continuation patterns are very similar to reversal signals, and if you are not aware of them, you might confuse the pattern and think that a standard reversal pattern had failed for you. The truth is that detailed analysis might show that it was never meant to signal a reversal in the first place, but was just a very similar continuation pattern.

This serves to illustrate the point about looking for other confirmation of the market sympathies before committing to the trade. For instance, if the second candle traces back to just over halfway in a Dark Cloud Cover, it is deemed to have made a reversal signal, and at just less than halfway, it is called a failing bearish attempt in a Bullish Thrusting pattern. The difference in the pattern is not that great, but the call is for the opposite result.

While a few candle patterns may be strong enough indications to trade confidently, it is rare that an experienced trader will base their decision on just the pattern, as you may notice from the case studies found throughout this book.

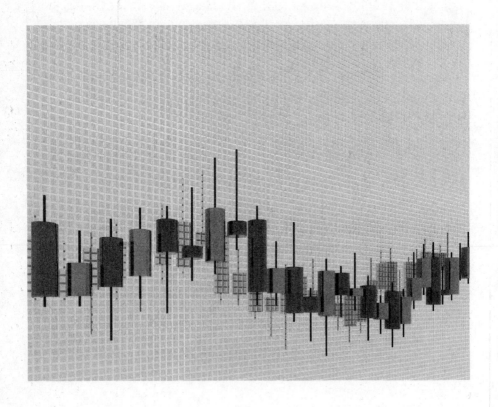

 # Candlestick Patterns — Three-Day Continuation Signals

Upside Tasuki Gap

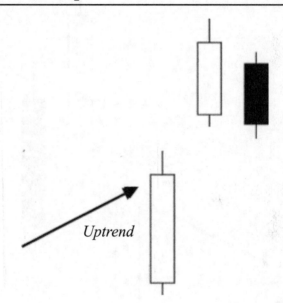

Uptrend

General Pattern

The Upside Tasuki Gap occurs in an uptrend. It requires a gap up between two, in-trend white candlesticks, which would suggest bullish strength. The progression is stalled by the third day, with a black candle that starts within the body of the second day and finishes lower in the gap, but not closing it.

Meaning

The meaning is simple. The gap is a strong indicator, which subsequently suffers a setback with the third day against the trend. As the gap is not closed, the pattern is regarded as just a breather in the upward rise of the price, and the continuation should be confirmed by other indications.

Upside Gap Three Methods

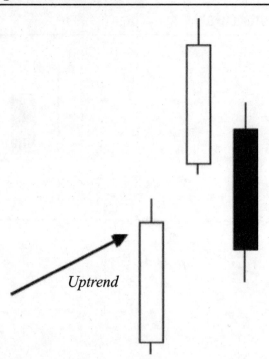

Uptrend

General Pattern

Similar to the Upside Tasuki Gap, the Upside Gap Three Methods pattern occurs in a strong uptrend. The upside gap between the first and second candlesticks, which are white and in trend, reflects the strength of the market. The third candle, a bearish line between the body of the second and the body of the first, closes the gap, and this is where it varies from the Tasuki version.

Meaning

The gap is an indication of the strong trend. The fact that the gap is closed immediately on the next day is not seen as weakness and is regarded as supporting the trend. The price at a gap will frequently become a support or resistance level in due course, but the trend is expected to continue for the moment.

Bullish Side By Side White Lines

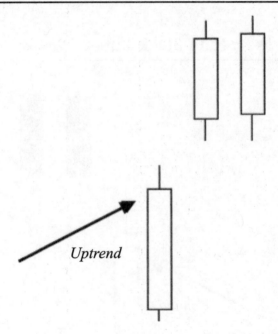

Uptrend

General Pattern

The Side By Side White Lines pattern can be seen in both an uptrend and a downtrend but is more likely in the bullish form. The bearish version is discussed later. The pattern involves a gap in the direction of the trend, followed by two white candlesticks that are similar with both opening around the same price.

The Bullish Side By Side White Lines pattern occurs in an uptrend, so there is a gap up after the first candle of the pattern, then two similar white lines.

Meaning

The Bullish Side By Side White Lines pattern has a gap up after the first candlestick, which emphasizes the trend. However, as the third opens and closes at similar levels to the second, this shows a pause in the rising prices. The psychology is that, although the open of the third candle was down at the level of the previous day, the bulls managed to rally the day up to the same level, which fought off the hesitancy. Thus, the interpretation of the pattern finishes as a bullish continuation containing a short period of consolidation.

Bullish Side By Side Black Lines

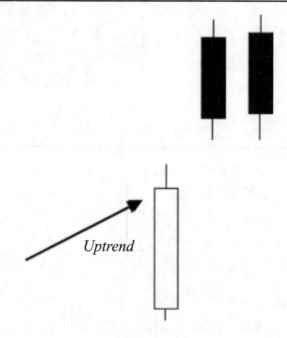

General Pattern

The Bullish Side by Side Black Lines pattern starts with a long white day in accordance with the prevalent uptrend. The second day gaps open well above the first day's close and trades lower, but does not fill the gap. The third day is similar, opening near the top of the second day and trading back down. Again, it does not fill the gap between the first and second candlesticks.

Meaning

This is a three-day continuation pattern, which, with confirmation, will show that the trend is continuing. The Bullish Side by Side Black Lines pattern starts with a long white body, which continues the current uptrend. Although the next two candles are black, signifying selling activity, they both open much higher than the first day, which implies a bullish strength, and neither comes back down to the level of the first candle. They are interpreted to be traders taking their profits, and the price is expected to rise after this.

Rest After Battle

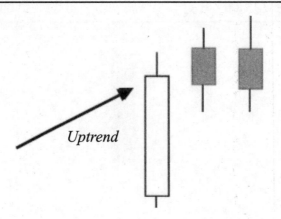

Uptrend

General Pattern

The Rest After Battle comes in an uptrend and has no bearish equivalent. It represents an allowance for a time of consolidation before the price continues upward. The first day is a long white candlestick, which should be significantly longer than the previous days' candles. The second and third days have short bodies, which can be either color.

Meaning

The second and third days are considered to be periods of rest before continuing the uptrend. The first candlestick shows the strength of the trend but exhausts the move temporarily. This pattern is typical of the type of uptrend that rises like a series of steps, with bursts of bullishness followed by a consolidation period.

Two conditions for this pattern are that the closing of the second day is above halfway of the first's real body and that the top of the real body is above the closing price of the first day, so that there is not too much weakness; however, the second day's low should be below the first day's high to avoid too much strength. The third day is limited to opening and closing within the range of the low and high of the second day.

Downside Taskui Gap

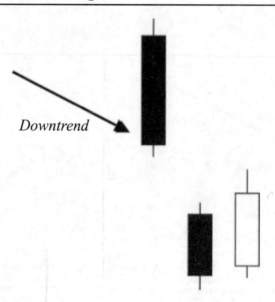

Downtrend

General Pattern

The Tasuki candlestick line is formed when the prices open higher than the previous day's close, then go on to close higher than the previous day's high, or the reverse for the Upside Tasuki Gap. This is the pattern of the second and third candles in this pattern.

Meaning

The pattern starts with an in-trend long black candle, and the second candle, also black, and thus in trend, opens with a gap down. The Tasuki is completed with the third white candle, which rallies to close in the gap but does not fill the gap.

The longstanding bearish trend is supported by the long black candle that starts this pattern. The gap down provides more evidence of the trend. The third candle is seen as profit taking, and because the gap has not been filled, it is assumed that the main trend will continue after this pause. Confirmation is recommended.

Downside Gap Three Methods

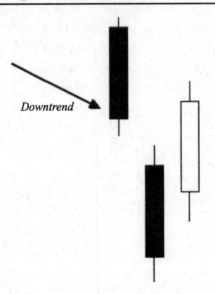

Downtrend

General Pattern

As with the Upside Gap pattern, the Downside Gap Three Methods pattern is usually seen in a strongly trending market and is similar to the Downside Tasuki Gap. The downward trend is continuing with two bearish black candles, the second gapping down from the first. The third day opens within the real body of the second and rallies to close within the real body of the first.

Meaning

The first two days are in keeping with the trend, and the third day opening within the second real body is unsurprising. The unexpected part of this pattern is the rally on the third day to close higher. Unlike the previous pattern, the Downside Tasuki Gap, the third day rallies sufficiently that the white body fills the gap between the first and second days, with its closing price above the first day's close. Nonetheless, this pattern is recognized as a continuation pattern.

The explanation for this is that the traders who held short positions in the stock rush to take their profits when they see the gap down between the first and second days, and this buying to cover their positions forces a temporary increase in the price. Confirmation is recommended, particularly as the ideas expressed are somewhat in conflict with the Tasuki perceptions.

Bearish Side By Side Black Lines

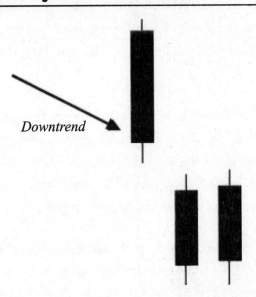

Downtrend

General Pattern

The Bearish Side By Side Black Lines occur in a downtrend. The first candle is in the trend, and the second day again gaps in the direction of the trend, as with the bullish pattern. The price falls during the day, closing as a black candle. The third candle opens much higher, about the same level as the second day, and repeats the price drop so that the second and third days' candlesticks are similar.

Meaning

The Bearish Side By Side Black Lines pattern starts with a long black day, which continues the downtrend currently in place. The second day, with a black candle opening much lower, emphasizes the downtrend. The only hesitation is that the third day opens back up again at the level of the second. However, this is attributed to some buying activity, and the price declines through the day, showing that the bears still retain control.

As mentioned under the bullish version, this pattern is rare. The market is in a downtrend, as evidenced by the first long black candlestick, and despite a gap down to the next, the following two days both produce white bullish candles. The white candles are similar, and both open around the same price.

The Bearish Side by Side White Lines pattern does not appear often, and the reasoning for it appearing as a continuation signal in a downtrend is a little more complex, involving market mechanics. The long black day starts the pattern, and the second day opens with a large gap downward, in trend. The market rallies all day but cannot close the gap.

On the third day, the market opens at the same position, and some traders buy to cover their short positions, as there seems to be resistance to the price dropping further. The buying to cover the shorts lifts the price again, but not enough to close the gap. If the rally is not strong and sufficient buying has taken place, then expect the price to continue downward.

● SAFETY ZONE ●

Most of these three candle formations are distinctive and do not show a steady progression in price. The reason for this is that a steady price progression is a common path for a continuing trend and does not need comment. These patterns encompass gaps and opposite color candles, and they may make you question the continuation of the trend. The patterns indicate that the trend should continue and, while remembering that nothing is certain in the markets, can provide some reassurance if you have a position that is in trend.

Candlestick Patterns — Four-Day Continuation Signals and Beyond

Rising Three Method

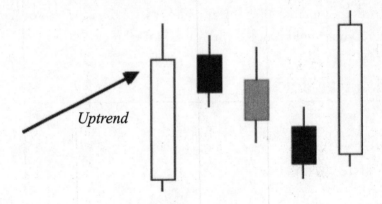

Uptrend

General Pattern

In an uptrend, the first candlestick is a long white day. The second, third, and fourth candlesticks are small bodied and progressively decline in price but, more importantly, do not go outside the high-low range of the first day, which is between the extremes of the shadows. These candles may be either color, with more strength to the pattern from black candles.

On the fifth day, the rally resumes with a long white day that opens above the previous close and goes on to close higher than the first day.

Meaning

This is considered to reflect the need for the market to take a break from the trend or to have a rest. Psychologically, it may be that the traders feel that the uptrend cannot continue. The middle candles may reflect this view, with some traders selling off and taking their profits. The fact that the reversal does not take hold, with the candles all having short bodies and not sinking below the first day, then inspires the bulls to take up the trend again and continue the uptrend with renewed vigor.

Some traders use the resting days to add to their position in the stock, and this can be a profitable move, given other indicators. Note that the first two candles are very similar to a Bearish Harami reversal pattern, differing only by the second day opening at a higher level than the first day's close; therefore, you should proceed with caution if taking this view.

Bullish Mat Hold

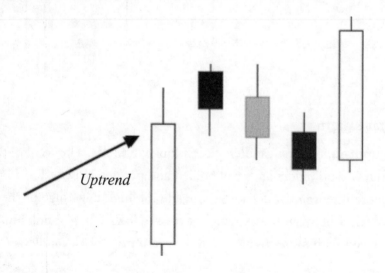

Uptrend

General Pattern

Similar to the Rising Three Method, but much rarer, the Bullish Mat Hold starts with a long white day in an uptrend, which is considered a strong.

The second day opens at a much higher price, and although it becomes a black candle, it is gapped up above the first. The third and fourth days are small bodied in a downward direction, with the third coming down to the first candle's real body. This is the difference from the Upside Gap Two Crows reversal pattern for these first three candles. The fifth day reasserts the uptrend with a long white day that closes above the previous candles.

Meaning

The long white day confirms the uptrend at the start of the pattern, and the gap open to the second day is also bullish. Even the closing price on this black candle is a new high. Over the third and fourth days, the bears are trying to take control and establish a reversal. By the time the fifth day comes, it is clear that the bearish trend has failed, and it opens higher and finishes much higher, starting the rally again with a long white day.

The three middle candles turn out to be just a rest in the continuing uptrend. This pattern, comparable with the Evening Star and the Two Crows reversal patterns, shows how separate confirmation of the state of the market can be useful in avoiding misinterpretation of the pattern.

Bullish Three Line Strike

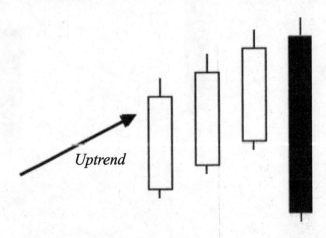

Uptrend

General Pattern

In an uptrend, the Bullish Three Line Strike is comprised of three white candlesticks in an upward progression followed on the fourth day by a long black day that opens at a higher level, but drops to close below the first day's opening price. The first part of the pattern is similar to Three White Soldiers in form, although that pattern is a reversal that occurs in a downtrend.

Meaning

The uptrend is shown to be continuing with good strength by the first three candles. The higher open on the fourth day is bullish but reverses to show a significant amount of selling off. This is regarded as a rest in the uptrend with traders taking profits, which moves the market strongly in the opposite direction for one day.

The interpretation put on this pattern is that the strong down day exhausts any bearish sentiment, and the uptrend will continue in the future.

Falling Three Method

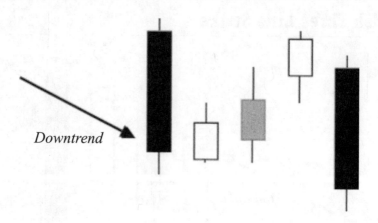

Downtrend

General Pattern

The bears are in control in a downward trending market, and the first candlestick confirms this. The next three candlesticks are small bodied and form a minor rally. They do not go outside the high-low range of the initial candle, however. The fifth candlestick resumes the downtrend with a long, strong black day that opens below the previous day's close and closes below the first day's close.

Meaning

The first candlestick is strong in the trend, reinforcing the market direction. The next three days run counter to that vein but are short bodied and therefore weaker than the first. This weakness is also shown by the fact that all three are within the extreme range of the first candle. These are regarded as the market taking a rest when the fifth day resumes the downtrend strongly. Look for firm action, as the market has been invigorated by the break, which assures traders that the downtrend is still in place.

Bearish Mat Hold

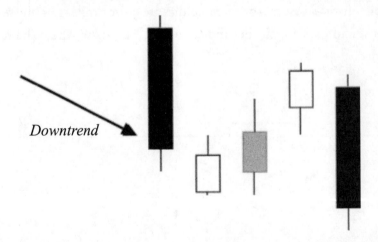

Downtrend

General Pattern

The downtrend continues on the first day of this pattern with a long black day. The second day gaps down, and although the day rallies to form a short white body, the close is lower than the first day's close, maintaining the gap, which is the difference from the Falling Three Method.

A weak rally continues, the third and fourth days having higher tops and higher bottoms, but they do not rise above the first day. The fifth day marks a resumption of the downtrend, with a long black day that opens below the close of the fourth day and closes below the rest of the pattern.

Meaning

The middle candles represent a time when the market pauses the downtrend and reconsiders the pricing of the security. These three candles do not close above the first candle's open, despite rallying, which indicates that the attempted reversal is failing, so the market resumes the downtrend on the fifth day. Compare this pattern to the Falling Three Method, of which this is a modified version.

Be aware that the first two or three candles are quite similar to some reversal patterns, and look for further indications to anticipate where the market is headed.

Bearish Three Line Strike

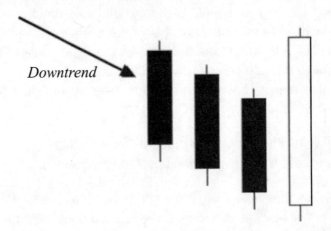

Downtrend

General Pattern

The Bearish Three Line Strike pattern consists of three long black candles in a downtrend, emphasizing the direction of the trend, with a gradual progression downward. These are followed by a long white candle, which opens at a gap down but rallies to close higher than the initial opening price of the pattern.

Meaning

This pattern is similar to the Three Black Crows pattern, which occurs in an uptrend as a reversal pattern. The anticipated result of both the Three Black Crows and the Bearish Three Line Strike is a downtrend. The fourth candle is usually explained as a result of the market taking a rest from the persistent bearish trend and may actually result from traders in a short position buying to cover their trades, having received a reasonable return to this point. This last candle is felt to have satisfied any bullish tendencies in the market, and the downtrend is expected to continue with the next day.

● SAFETY ZONE ●

There are lessons to be learned from the descriptions of these continuation patterns. Several of them refer to tired markets and the market taking a breather from the trend. In these patterns, the balance of probability is that the trend will continue, but in other patterns given before, the tiredness has sometimes been deemed sufficient to cause a reversal.

You may wonder how you can distinguish between these two cases with opposite results. Obviously, a wrong decision can result in a loss.

If you had no other indication, you might trade for a reversal. Of course, you will either be right or wrong. If the reversal does not happen, you can see that quickly and get out of the position for a small loss. If it does happen, you will often make several times what you were prepared to lose. Even if you choose at random, using excellent money management can cause you to avoid losing the bulk of your capital and have the possibility of good returns.

Plainly, you want to trade for the highest probability of success, but if you are prepared to be disciplined in your exit from a losing trade and apply good money management, you will be able to control your losses and make a profit. The entry to a trade is just one part of trading profitably.

Application of
Candlestick Charting

Having read through the descriptions of the candlestick patterns, you may have one of two reactions. One reaction may be that of confidence and readiness to set up your account and start trading, following the advice for each pattern that you can find. The other reaction may be feeling overwhelmed by so many variations and wondering how you can ever apply them.

Those who cannot wait to get started would do well to quell their enthusiasm and read the next chapters for help setting off on the right foot. Without applying some control, it is easy to be misled by emotions, knowledge, and the markets, and a trading career is quickly finished when you run out of money.

Readers wondering whether trading using candlestick charting is such a good idea and perhaps feeling like giving up in the face of such complication and detail, should also read the following chapters to get a sense of perspective on the task ahead. Learn to use the wisdom of the ancients and apply candlesticks to your efforts.

The Place for Candlesticks

Candlestick charting provides an insight into the psychology of the markets. It is better suited for trading as opposed to investing — that is, it can help with identifying short-term price expectations, but it has nothing to add to consideration of where to put your money for a long period. As such, it is a tool to use with technical analysis and not with fundamental analysis, as discussed in Chapter 4.

You can trade well without using candlestick charting, and many people do. Learning about candlesticks will not provide an instant inside track to fast profits. Successful trading requires study and can involve many different techniques. Computer programs routinely generate perhaps 100 different indicators for any stock price chart, and the choice of which to use can be a monumental challenge with no one correct solution as different indicators work better in different situations.

In this chapter, we will look at the technical application of the charts.

The Limitations of Candlesticks

Candlesticks can be very powerful, but with the wrong approach, they can also be useless or even misleading. They must first be considered in the context of the trend in which they appear. If you were following the pattern chapters closely, you will have noted that most of the patterns were associated with a trending chart, and some patterns are even interpreted with opposite meanings, depending on the prevailing trend.

This is not the only potential problem with candlesticks. You also have likely noticed that some candlestick patterns are called stronger than others — for instance, the Kicking pattern is considered powerful. Consider what this means: The price will go up or down. If the pattern is powerful, the price is likely to go in the predicted direction most of the time when you see the pattern. If the pattern is not considered so strong, the price may not go in the intended direction so frequently. All that the pattern interpretations are saying is that the particular example is more likely than not to go in the stated direction, and they do not necessarily relate much in terms of how large the move will be or whether that is a profitable thing to know.

This may be a disappointment to you if you were looking for the mythical "Holy Grail" that seems to be the goal of many short-term traders. It is one reason that you have to be prepared to lose (moderately) while making money trading, and you need to consider other indicators, or pointers, to add weight to the decisions you make. The concept of taking other indicators into account is called "filtering," and the prospective stocks are screened with conventional indicators to see how likely the moves suggested by the candlestick patterns are to come to fruition. The markets have no notion of what they "ought" to do. The patterns work on the balance of probability and are based on the aggregate expected reaction of normal, emotional human beings who are trading. The patterns do not magically define and force the market to respond in a particular way.

The Advantages of Candlesticks

It is worth considering how candlesticks can bring a unique insight into the markets and provide guidance that is not available from other analysis. Consider the information with which we can arm ourselves to steer our trading activities. The indicators that are available on the charts are based on historic information, as they cannot be based on what has not happened yet. The historic information goes back over several time periods.

For instance, moving averages are often part of the decision making. By definition, these may reflect the last six or eight days of prices for trading signals, and perhaps 40 or more days for trend information. Calculated indicators are not much more up to date, yet we use them as the basis for a trading decision today.

Candlesticks are much more recent than that. Comprising typically just a few days, the candlestick pattern provides a trading indication that is much faster and thus more likely to partake in the maximum swing in price. While the technical indicators may be able to say that the time is near, the candles can tell you that the time is now.

The correct, profitable, and safe way to use candlestick knowledge is in collaboration with indicators chosen from the number available with Western charting techniques — that is, using filtering.

Blended Candle

The concept of a blended candle is simple, and it provides you with a quick guide to the meanings of patterns. Steve Nison is credited with inventing the name "blended candle," which is very descriptive of the process.

The idea is that you regard two or more days as one and draw the appropriate candlestick, using the high and low range of the combined period, the opening price on the first day, and the closing price on the last. In other words, you are compressing the price activity of several days together.

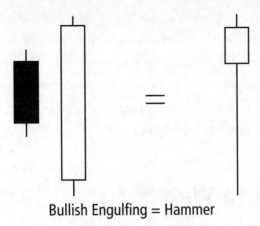

Bullish Engulfing = Hammer

In this example, you can see how it works. The pattern on the left blends to form the candle on the right. The Bullish Engulfing two-day pattern becomes a Hammer when it is compressed into a blended form. The opening price for the two days is the top of the first bearish candle, and the closing price is the top of the second long white bullish candle. Drawing the equivalent candle body results in the small white body near the top of the range. The range, forming the shadows, is just the extreme range of both days.

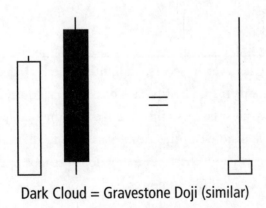

Dark Cloud = Gravestone Doji (similar)

Here is a second example where the Dark Cloud pattern blends to almost form a Gravestone Doji or perhaps part of a Shooting Star pattern. Both of these patterns are bearish reversals that come in an uptrend.

The blended candle system does not always produce equivalents; you will even find some patterns that blend to form a candle with the opposite interpretation. These are usually patterns where it is particularly recommended that the reversal signal is confirmed by watching the action on the next day. It is a fascinating exercise to cut out the detail to reduce the meaning of a pattern to its basics.

Patterns to Watch

With so many patterns, some more rare than others, this section highlights the fundamental patterns that keep recurring and that you will want to commit to memory.

Ask different candlestick experts, and they will probably give you different answers on how many candlestick patterns are the major figures. I have seen up to 21 mentioned as essential, and others list only seven. Twelve is a common number of candles named as major. The following are the ones that I have found are key.

Doji

First, the doji, whenever it occurs, should be watched closely. The most money is to be made from identifying a price reversal quickly, and the doji is the candle that most conveys the message that the market psychology is in turmoil and that no clear direction exists among the traders. The only exception to that is if the chart has many doji, perhaps from being thinly traded, in which case it loses its power.

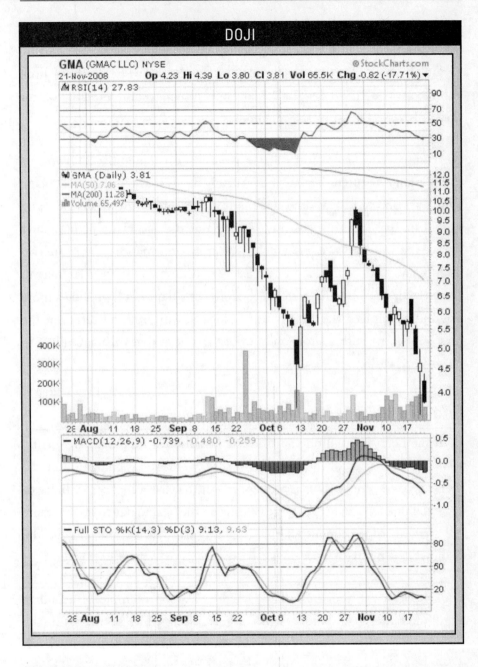

Here is an example where the doji do not have much significance, especially in the August section on the left side. You will see many doji or near doji, having short real bodies, with very little discernible price movement. If you look more closely, specifically at the bottom of the main chart, you will see a skyscraper-like horizon, and this is the charting of the volume. The actual numbers are on the left. There is very little volume showing until September, and this provides some explanation for the shortness of most of the real bodies.

You can see that the greatest volume by far was on September 24, two bars to the right of September 22, and that this day was also a short real body. This was followed by a rapid decline in price, which shows that it was a significant day. In retrospect, it is easy to name this as a Hanging Man, and the open on the following day being lower is confirmation. There are two bullish days prior to this day, but it is far from clear that there was a rally to be reversed. The opening price on the following day would provide a more sure indication that the market was headed downward, and certainly, the massive volume with a short body would alert you that this period was to be watched closely.

Engulfing Patterns

Both the Bearish Engulfing and Bullish Engulfing patterns are frequently seen, and the nature of the form shows that the market is being dominated by the second candle. This is a major signal that has a high probability of success. Look especially for a large volume on the second day to demonstrate the strength of sentiment. If the engulfing candlestick also engulfs the shadows and/or engulfs previous days too, then the signal is stronger.

Look back at the previous chart. There is a good example of a bullish engulfing pattern on October 13th, where a long white body engulfs the previous day. This pattern also shows good trading volume, which lends more reliability to it, and indeed, the next day gapped open. Looking at the RSI at the top of the chart, or the stochastic oscillator at the bottom provides further evidence that the rally was due, as both these indicators show that the stock was heavily oversold.

Star Patterns

This heading covers several different patterns. The common thread is that a Spinning Top candle, the actual Star, is gapped away from a long-bodied candle in trend. The Spinning Top, a short real body, shows the indecision that has entered the market, possibly because the gap has overstretched the comfort zone of the trades that were following the trend.

The Star is more significant if it gaps clear of the range, rather then just having the real bodies separate and if the Star candlestick is a doji, instead of just a short body. The Star reversal is confirmed by the next candle, or the pattern has failed.

Harami

The Harami is often seen, and usually, the second, smaller candle is the opposite color, but it does not have to be. There are several pointers that give the Harami a better probability of success in reversing the trend.

If the second candle is the opposite color, then the longer it is, the stronger the signal. Looking at the second candle's location, relative to the first, if it is further along in the direction of the reversal, this strengthens the likelihood of a reversal taking place. The Harami's strength lies in it belying the indication and direction of the first candlestick by failing to progress the price beyond the range of that real body, so the color is less significant, although it is an indication of the strength and thus how much trust you should put in the signal.

Dark Cloud Cover and Piercing Line

These complementary patterns are considered to be significant by some commentators. Although the two candlesticks are relatively similar in price position, they are of opposite colors, and this introduces the idea of examining where the psychology of the traders is going during the day.

For instance, the Dark Cloud Cover consists of a bullish long white candle in an uptrend, followed by a long black candle where the body is higher than the first but overlaps at least half. To form this pattern means that on the second day, the price gapped up at the open. During the day, the price fell significantly until it was only just above the previous day's opening price. This long candle shows appreciable sentiment for the price to decline, as happens after a gap up, which often seems to tire out the market.

Other Patterns

While you may want to commit other patterns to memory, particularly if you intend day trading and do not have the time to keep looking them up, the fundamentals should be clear to you now, and these are the main patterns that you need to know. Once you appreciate the way in which the trading of the day is revealed to you in each candlestick, you are able to make much better trading decisions.

Candlestick Confirmations

By now, you will have noticed that much emphasis is being placed on looking for confirmation of the candlestick pattern interpretations before trading on them. This is not to be taken as a criticism of the accuracy of candlestick charting methods, as they have become very refined over the years, but it is a way to improve your trading percentages to maximize the potential profit that you can make. After all, it is naïve to expect the market to reverse if there is no evident pressure from traders for it to do so, and you would find such trades eating into any profits that you get from better performing trades.

This observation raises the question of which other indicators you should use for confirmation — after all, there are many of them, as a glance at any charting program will affirm. The trading experts who contributed to the success stories in this book were asked, and their favorite indicators included: stochastics, relative strength index, moving average convergence, divergence, guppy multiple moving average, count back line analysis, and intraday momentum index. These indicators are mainly oscillators that will give you an idea of whether the stock is overbought, oversold, or in the middle.

Other conventional technical analysis tools mentioned included: support and resistance, moving averages, volume, volatility, Bollinger Bands, and

Fibonacci retracements and extensions. Several of these can be used for price targets, as well as identifying likely turning points. Of course, you do not have to use all of these in your trading, and you would be well advised to restrict yourself to two or three, at the most. However, you may want to look first at these, as well as other indicators, to see which fit in best with your style and, most important, work effectively and reliably.

Moving Averages

One of the fundamental technical charting tools is the moving average. This actually represents a whole range of tools that can provide indication of trends and of trading triggers.

The simple moving average usually has a number associated with it that refers to the number of recent time periods that are averaged together to get the value for the day. The simple moving average is an average value that is recalculated each day, giving a value that is connected to the previous one to draw a line. If you use the simple moving average (SMA) over many periods, such as 50 or 200, it will plot on the chart as a fairly smooth line that indicates the trend — up or down.

The trend can be important in interpreting a candlestick pattern, and this is a simple, effective way to be sure that you are looking at the pattern in the correct way. This is a basic function that you can find on all charting software, including Web sites, such as **finance.yahoo.com** or **moneycentral. msn.com**. Even on their simple charts, you can choose to use candlesticks and select from a large range of other indicators.

With a large period, the line is quite smooth. If you experiment with shorter periods —that is, a lower number — the line becomes closer to the current price. This can be used to give a simple trading signal, as when a stock price crosses the line; it indicates that the trend is changing and can be a sign of a time to trade. This is inevitably a lagging signal, and so is not often used, with many traders preferring a more sophisticated system.

You can also use an exponential moving average (EMA), which is a moving average that is calculated with a bias for the more recent figures. Another trading technique with moving averages is to plot two lines, such as the EMA 5 and EMA 6, for five and six days respectively, and consider it a trading trigger when the lines cross, subject to appropriate trends being in place.

A moving average can be useful in providing a support level in an uptrend. With an appropriate choice of number of periods, the price will often seem to use the moving average as a support line, fluctuating up and down, but seldom crossing it. When the price approaches this moving average, you should look for a bullish reversal pattern to capture the bounce up from the line with a winning trade.

Oscillators

In trading jargon, there are "oscillators" — literally, technical indicators that oscillate between two boundary values — and these are commonly used to determine whether a particular stock is oversold or overbought. If a stock is oversold, the meaning is that it has been sold so much that it may need to recover some of its value, or rally. If it is overbought, that means that everybody seems to have been enthusiastically buying it up, and it may be due for some buyers' regret, or some selling off, with the consequent loss in value. As such, oscillators can be used to make or support your trading decisions and warn you if the candle pattern is not in keeping with the general view toward the stock, in which case, you should not trade.

Oscillators are usually based on the momentum of the stock price movement. The momentum is a measure of whether a particular trend is running out of steam. As with all technical analysis, the stock prices do not know about the indicators that we use, and therefore, may not comply with what they are supposed to do when we get a particular value. The indicators are used and have been developed to give an indication that works much of the time, though, so with a suitable money-management strategy to avoid large losses, they can be part of the basis for a trading decision.

There are many available oscillators, as you will see if you look at the options on any charting program. More have been developed to try to overcome perceived shortcomings with those available and to get an edge over other traders. None are perfect, and the ones looked at here, mentioned by the participants in the case studies, do not preclude the use of any alternative that you may favor.

Indicators will normally go in a similar direction to the price chart. If the price is rising, the oscillator line will also be going upward. When the price drops so does the oscillator. As all oscillators do not exactly track each other, there will be deviations to this idea, but you will find that it applies the majority of the time. Consequently, if the price diverges from the indicator, you should be careful and watch closely to see if the stock does something unexpected.

Stochastic Oscillator

This was invented by Dr. George Lane in the 1970s and was very popular in the 1990s when it was almost considered the Holy Grail of trading. The power of the computer is used to perform the necessary calculations, and standard charting applications allow you to simply use it without getting involved with the details. You should appreciate its derivation, however, so that you can be aware of its uses and possible limitations. The interesting point about the stochastic oscillator is that it does not just work on single price points for each day but takes into account the different values seen during the day. In other words, it relates the closing price to the full range of prices seen.

When prices are rising, the closing prices tend to be toward the top of the range of prices for the day; if prices are dropping, the tendency is to close near the lower end. The calculation uses the closing price, along with the lowest low and the highest high seen in the previous period, which may typically be 14 days or periods to generate values.

The indicator generates two variables, which are plotted as lines. These are called the %K and the %D. These letters are universal today and have an arbitrary derivation from the fact that Lane was experimenting with many indicators at the time, labeling them alphabetically, and these were the ones that he found worked best.

The %K is the oscillator line per se, and the %D is a signal line that comes from plotting the average of %K. As stated above, the %K is often calculated for 14 time periods, and the %D is a three-day moving average of %K, but these values can be altered to try and improve the predictive performance.

As a further complication, there are two variations on the stochastic oscillator. That described above is the "fast" oscillator. The "slow" oscillator takes a smoothed oscillator line for %K and smooths it more for the %D. With the common default values, the slow %K is a three-day average of the fast %K, which means it is numerically the same as the fast %D.

With this much background to the oscillator, you may be happy to realize that the function is pre-programmed, and you do not need to change the default values unless you want to try and hone the performance. Your main decision, therefore, comes down to whether you prefer the fast or the slow oscillator, and you should make this determination by looking at the historic performance of each on the stock you are considering.

Typically, the stochastics are plotted in a separate graph below the main chart and have a normalized value from zero to one hundred. Lines are usually drawn at 20 and 80. When the indicator drops below 20, the stock is considered oversold. A value over 80 is an indication of the stock being overbought.

If you were to trade on the basis of the stochastic oscillator alone, there are two distinct ways in which it can be used. It is not usual to trade based on just one factor as most traders require a second, non-related indication that the trade is likely to succeed to improve the probability.

The first way that you could use the stochastic oscillator is to buy when the oscillator line has gone below 20 and is starting back up. The stock is indicated as being oversold when the oscillator is below 20, which means that it should be due for a rally. Sell when the oscillator rises to above 80, indicating that the stock is overbought and may stall its rise.

You may also trade short using this technique, waiting for the oscillator to drop through the 80 percent line before taking a short position and closing your trade when it hits the 20 percent.

Another common method to determine trading opportunities with the stochastic oscillator is to take the trigger point of the %K and %D lines crossing. When the %K line rises up through the %D line—this is taken to be a bullish indication—you should buy the stock; with the %K dropping through the %D, you have a signal to sell.

If you want to use stochastics to give confirmation of what the candlestick patterns are indicating, then the easiest way is to look for a bullish reversal pattern when the stochastic is below 20 and buy when you see the pattern. If you are interested in going short on the stock, you would wait until the stochastic was over 80, indicating it was overbought and ready for a correction; then, wait for a bearish reversal pattern to trigger the trade.

Relative Strength Index (RSI)

J. Welles Wilder was the developer of the RSI indicator, which expresses the relative strength of the current price movement on a scale from zero to 100. It is important to note that this has nothing to do with the strength of a stock relative to another or to the market sector; it just compares the strength of different periods for the same stock.

The RSI is often taken over a period of 14 days, and the number of days or periods can usually be set for whatever you find works best with the securities you are trading. Wilder used 14, as he felt that it worked well with the cyclical nature of the markets. For the levels of significance, Wilder preferred to use the levels of 30 and 70 for gauging the sentiment of the market with his indicator.

The RSI takes the average upward move, compared with the average downward move, over the last number of periods, and charts the result from zero to 100. It would be unusual to approach those extremes, and the values that are significant are 25–35 and 65–75. Some people use different levels for different types of security, and it is worth exploring what works best for your style of trading.

The RSI is generally not considered as accurate as the stochastic oscillator, but it gives an easy reference to find times that appear oversold or overbought, when it would be worthwhile to watch for the appropriate candlestick patterns to signal a trading entry. As with the stochastic, a common practice is to look for a stock that the oscillator indicates is oversold or overbought and monitor the stock each day for the candlestick pattern to trigger a trade.

Moving Average Convergence Divergence (MACD)

Developed by Gerald Appel to address apparent problems with using simple moving averages, the MACD is based on moving averages but considers whether two moving averages are converging to or diverging from each other. Instead of simply considering when two moving averages cross as a signal for trading, this indicator gauges the rate at which the averages are coming together or moving apart.

As explained, moving averages are a lagging indicator, only reacting and signaling after the best time to get into a trade. While this still applies to any indicator calculated from historic values, the MACD tries to speed the detection of a possible trade. It does this by anticipating the crossing of the lines by looking at the convergence. Before they cross, they must converge, or come together, first.

However, if you wait until they converge, all you have is another way of showing the crossing. When the lines have fully converged, they are actually crossing. The trick that Appel invented was to highlight how much the convergence was varying by plotting a moving average of the convergence-divergence on the graph and seeing where it crossed the indicator itself, which almost magically seems to anticipate the moving average lines crossing.

The MACD is typically plotted on a graph under the price chart and has two lines. The MACD line itself is calculated from the difference between two exponential moving averages, typically for 12 and 26 days or periods. The other line is a smooth line made from averaging the MACD line using the exponential moving average (EMA) with a period of typically nine days. This is called the signal line.

There are several possible uses for the MACD indicator in short-term trading. It can be used as a trend confirmation by noting that when the MACD line is above the signal line, the price is trending upward. The opposite also applies. If the MACD is below the signal line, then the price is falling, and you should only consider short trades, which are trades that make money when the value drops.

When the MACD line diverges from the signal line, it is likely that the stock will become overbought or oversold, and it should be watched. The same is true if the direction of the line deviates from the direction of the price line, as this is not a condition that will remain for long.

The crossing of the signal line and the MACD line are often taken as triggers for trading. When the MACD rises above the signal line, this crossover can be taken as the time to buy the stock, and when it passes down through the signal line, it is time to sell. Some other recommendations are to buy when the MACD rises through the center line and sell when it drops back down into negative territory. The MACD is a flexible concept, and how you use it depends on your trading style and the characteristics of the securities you are trading. It is best to back-test — that is, check it against historical data — to see what works well for your situation.

In the context of reinforcing a candlestick pattern's indication of a trading opportunity, you can look for one of these possible signals occurring at the same time as a candle pattern that would support the reversal.

Another approach is simply to see when the MACD is in its upper range, as this should indicate that the stock is overbought. When a bearish reversal pattern occurs, you can short the stock to make profits when the price falls. If the MACD moves toward the lower end to show an oversold situation, wait for a bullish reversal candlestick pattern and buy the stock.

Guppy Multiple Moving Average (GMMA)

Not surprisingly, it was Daryl Guppy who said that he used the Guppy Multiple Moving Average in conjunction with his assessment of candlestick patterns. The GMMA is available on the industry-standard MetaStock® charting and analysis software and on many other programs. It attempts to identify the interplay between investor and trader psychology so that the strength of the underlying trend may be better understood. Here is Guppy's case study, where he talks about the indicators that he has developed.

CASE STUDY: DARYL GUPPY

Box 40043, Casuarina, Northern Territory, Australia, 0811. Phone: +61 8 89270061; Fax: +61 8 89270125; china@guppytraders.com.

Offices and staff in Darwin, Kuala Lumpur (+60 321697733), Singapore (+65 68663339), and Beijing (+86 13120148738).

Daryl Guppy is CNBC Asia "Squawk Box" technical analyst commentator and is often known as "the chart man."

He is recognized globally for the quality of his analysis and has a weekly **www.CNBC.com** column — Charting Asia. He actively trades equities and associated derivatives markets, including CFDs. He is the author of *The 36 Strategies of The Chinese For Financial Traders, Trend Trading*, and seven other trading books. He has developed several leading technical indicators used by traders in stock, derivative, and currency markets. Guppy is a regular contributor for financial magazines and media in Singapore, Malaysia, China, Australia, and the U.S. He oversees the production of weekly analysis and trading newsletters for the Singapore/Malaysia market, the mainland China, India, and Australian markets.

He is recognized as a leading expert on China markets. He is in demand as a speaker in Asia, China, Europe, and Australia.

CASE STUDY: DARYL GUPPY

What type of trading do you use candlesticks with — what markets and time periods?

I use candlesticks mainly for trading in Asian markets. This is the chart display most commonly used in these markets, so it's useful to understand the way other traders are analyzing markets and making trading decisions. I use candles for end-of-day trading and also for intraday trading of derivatives. I find this gives a better visual understanding of developing momentum and the velocity of trading.

It is very important to ensure you are trading with classic candle construction rather than candles that are constructed as an extension of Gann continuation charts. The candle signals given on Gann continuation-style candle charts are not the same as those generated with classic candle signals derived from Japanese charting analysis.

When and how did you start getting interested in trading?

I have been trading markets as my primary source of income since 1990. I do not manage other people's money or run a fund; I trade my own account. I started trading from a very remote location in the Australian outback. The only up-to-date information I had was daily price activity. I learned to understand the behavior of other people in the market by applying chart analysis. I am a chartist, and I see a price chart as a record of the behavioral characteristics of the market. I trade the psychology of market behavior. I started trading because it was the most efficient way to generate growth using a small amount of capital. It remains the most effective way to grow capital and manage risk.

Did you use candlestick charts from the start of your trading? If not, how much difference do you think they made to your trades when you learned to interpret them?

I started using bar charts, and I still use bar charts for a considerable part of my trading and analysis. Each charting method and display method has its own set of advantages and disadvantages. When you combine several different methods of display for price action, it can be used to improve analysis. The main difference is that by switching between the display options, you can identify different types of opportunity that may be more appropriate for the stock or instrument you are trading. In certain time frames, particularly intraday, I will always use candles rather than a bar chart.

CASE STUDY: DARYL GUPPY

Do you enter a trade on the basis of a candlestick pattern only — always, sometimes, or never?

I rarely enter a trade on the basis of a candle pattern alone. This pattern may alert me to a particular type of opportunity, but I am looking for weight of evidence to help decide between competing opportunities. In intraday trading, I am looking for particular relationships to trigger entry conditions, particularly in momentum style trades. In this situation, I will use candles and candle relationships because there is no time to assess weight of evidence as the trade develops.

What other indicators do you use in conjunction with candlesticks if you want confirmation? Which do you find work best in combination with candle signals?

I apply Guppy Multiple Moving Average (GMMA) analysis, count back line analysis, and classic pattern analysis in trade selection and management. Candle signals fall within the context of broader market and opportunity analysis. On an intraday basis, the initial trade identification starts with GMMA analysis. Candle analysis is used to identify exact entry points and entry conditions.

Do you use and find filters, such as price or volume, effective in assisting selection of worthwhile candlestick patterns?

Volume assessment is one of the final steps in trade selection. The character of volume and volume/price relationships provides a guide to price manipulation, stability of trends, development of rallies, and other related trading features. On an intraday chart, it is the velocity of volume that helps to confirm candles and candle pattern signals.

The application of candle pattern relationships is part of a weight of evidence approach where each potential trade is filtered through a series of analysis steps.

CASE STUDY: DARYL GUPPY

There are many named candlestick patterns. Do you find that you only focus on a few, and if so, which?

The validity and reliability of candle patterns and relationships will depend on many factors. This includes changes in market conditions and the instrument being traded. The patterns that are most effective with stocks in a bull market may be less effective and reliable in a derivative instrument in the same market condition. When market conditions change, for instance, where volatility increases, the type of candle patterns that are most reliable also change.

The challenge with all trading is not to identify the best method. The challenge is to identify the most reliable combination that applies to the current market conditions and to know when to adjust those methods.

The successful candle relationships we use now are different from those we used several years ago. In each market condition, we focus on using a few candle patterns that have a high level of reliability in the selected market condition and in relation to the instrument being traded.

Is this just because you find them the most effective, or is it also because of other factors, such as how often they occur, for example?

Frequency of pattern occurrence is not a guide to reliability. False signals can appear more often than genuine signals. We must always assess reliability on patterns and behavior in relation to the instrument we are trading. We must also assess reliability in relation to the market condition we are trading, and this may mean assessing the pattern in a selected period. Back-testing over a data set extending back 100 years does not yield useful results. Indicators must be back-tested against periods that most closely resemble the current market conditions.

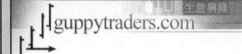
guppytraders.com

Commonly, a trader would use the relationship between moving averages of different periods, perhaps including the crossings, to follow underlying trends and short-term movements. The GMMA uses groups of averages, which allows further information and inferences to be drawn from the chart. Because it deals in so many averages, it relies on the computer to provide the needed calculations.

Guppy's concern was whether a rally was short term or if it was part of a trend. In other words, his indicator was designed to show clearly the difference between long-term and intermediate-term price moves, and it asserts that where traders lead the prices changing, whether up or down, they need investors; in other words, they need the long-term money to follow so that the values can be maintained.

The GMMA uses a group of short-term averages — exponential moving averages based on three, five, ten, twelve, and fifteen days. When the distance between these is small, or compressed, then there is good agreement between traders on the price. If some traders were to think that the price should be different, then the action of their trading with that in mind would cause the lines to separate, revealing the disagreement.

Guppy took a further step with this theme, plotting a group of longer-term exponential averages for 30, 35, 40, 45, 50, and 60 days on the same chart. For these, when the average lines expand out, it shows that there is pressure among longer-term investors to change the price as they perceive a different value to the stocks. Thus, a strong underlying trend is evidenced by a spread in these lines.

Use of the GMMA includes looking at the spread in each set of averages, the relationship between the two groups and the crossovers between them. Guppy has a Web site, **www.guppytraders.com**, where you can discover more information about this concept.

Count Back Line Analysis (CBL)

Guppy also developed CBL, which is a volatility-based indicator. As with the GMMA, it is involved in verifying the existence and strength of a trend. In this case, he harnesses the day-to-day fluctuations to set the line position, and it can find service as a stop-loss indicator and as a trend-break indicator, showing when the prices move out of the expected range.

Further details on this concept are also available from Guppy's Web site.

Intraday Momentum Index (IMI)

The intraday momentum index is an oscillator with oversold and overbought lines at 30 percent and 70 percent, and, as with other oscillators, it can be used to filter stocks for selection. The core of the IMI is consideration and comparison of the length of the real bodies of the candlesticks—the difference between the opening and closing prices—without study of the shadows or wicks.

The indicator actually compares the total size of the bullish white bodies to the total size of the bearish black bodies over the past period, typically 14 days. If there were many white bodies compared with the number of black, or if the white bodies were long and the black were short, then the value would be high. In theory, with many long white bodies and a few short black bodies, the value could approach 100 percent.

Support and Resistance

We touched on the concept of support and resistance earlier, particularly with the tweezer and matching patterns. The concept is fairly clear: The support level is at a price that you do not expect the stock to go below — it provides support for the price — and the resistance level makes it difficult for the stock price to go above that level. They are not in a permanent position, and they are not beyond being breached by what is called a breakout, but often, they seem to work for a time.

Sometimes, the price of a stock will seem to go between two fixed values for some time. Each time the price rises to the high level and then retreats, that action serves to provide more justification for believing that the resistance value is well defined and will work again; when the stock drops to the lower level but not below, then the support level is proved.

One form of successful trading is to buy when the stock reaches the support, sell when it touches resistance and do so repeatedly for as long as the stock is well behaved. In this case, a failure of the price to stay above the support level would indicate that you should sell immediately to cut your losses, and the money management chapter discusses how to minimize losses.

Another example of using support and resistance levels was explained by Nicholas Darvas as what he called a "box theory." While the price of a stock moved between set levels, he regarded it as being in a box. Should it go outside, he knew that it was on the way to setting higher levels of support and resistance or a higher box. His methods used this certainty that he felt about predicting the price movements with much obvious success.

This application of support and resistance applies to horizontal lines on the price charts, and sometimes, you will find that they occur at psychologically significant numbers. For instance, every whole $5 or $10, you may notice some effect on the fluidity of the price movement. This graphically illustrates how trading is a mental game at which you are playing against other people, rather than just seeking a coolly calculated, technically correct solution.

In the context of using candlestick patterns, the position of the support and resistance lines and the price approaching them will give information that can be used to agree or disagree with the message of the patterns. If you see a bearish reversal pattern, and the price is nearly at resistance, then there is a strong indication that the reversal will happen as indicated by the candlesticks.

Trendlines

There is an alternate and equally valid way to look at support and resistance levels, and this depends on the individual stock's behavior. If the stock is trending, then the levels can be sloped to follow the trend. Often, such lines are drawn by joining just two or three of the extreme lows and extreme highs and projecting them onward. The routine fluctuations in price as the average value rises will be contained by the lines, and any move to go outside is a warning that the trend may be changing.

In a similar vein to the support and resistance, you may also wish to use these trendlines to assist in working out whether the stock is at a point where the message of a candlestick pattern can be believed. Instead of just trading on the basis of the pattern, using confirmation from another analysis will provide a valuable safeguard against overtrading and help you avoid many early stop-loss exits from your trades.

Trendlines are not quite as simple as they appear, even though they are easy to understand. A trendline is a straight line that extends from the beginning of a trend to the end. It can be drawn on a printed paper chart, or it may be added with software on a computer chart. The problem arises when you try and rationalize exactly where they start and stop.

Sometimes, the location of a trendline will be obvious, and it can be readily drawn. Other charts, although obviously trending, may prove more difficult. The trend may depend on the scale of the chart that you are examining, as a stock that trends cleanly in one scale may undergo large fluctuations in another scale that make the line hard to draw. There may even be several locations that are arguably as valid.

The drawing of a trendline can be quite valuable, as you do not want to buy a share unless the price is increasing. The scale on which you base your decision is critical for this, as a longer timescale that shows an uptrend might work well for investors, but on a daily scale, the trend could be down, making it unsuitable for short-term trading profits. Many patterns require that you identify a trend, and as candlestick charting is equally applicable to all timescales, you must take care to ensure the appropriateness to your trading requirements.

Another point about trendlines is that they are often not obvious until after the whole chart has been drawn and looked at in retrospect. In general, you will try to connect from the start of the trend to the present so that the line seems a good representation of the price slope, while ignoring the odd spike that may be an exception, and your eye will be a good guide to the "best" location. You should be ready to change the location of the line as time progresses and you receive new information that is in conflict with the old line.

Although with practice, you can make a reasonable estimate of the trendline location, there are a couple of tricks that you can use to formalize the drawing so that you are not distorting it in favor of your desired outcome.

For an uptrend, you should connect the lowest low with the low before the highest high. As new highs are made, change the line to connect to the latest low before the new high, and when new highs are no longer being made, consider that trendline finished. For a downtrend, you can draw the line in a similar way, connecting the highest high to the high before the latest low, until new lows are no longer being made, and the trend may be considered to have changed.

Bollinger Bands

A further refinement on the idea of support and resistance lines giving values that you do not expect to go outside is found in the Bollinger Bands. These are calculated lines on each side of the price, so you do not have the subjectivity of drawing trendlines. What they do is capture the trend and the volatility at any particular time and provide a reference that you can use for more analysis.

Bollinger Bands are available on most charting software. They were invented by John Bollinger, and they give you a visual image of whether a price is high or low. There is an upper band, over the price, and when the price rises close to this, it can be considered high. There is a lower band, and if the price drops down to this, then it is relatively low. Bollinger Bands also include a middle band, and if the price is close to this, then it is considered about right with little pressure to go up or down.

If you have done any statistical study, you may know of the idea of standard deviation, which is a mathematical measure of how much variation there is in a value. This is used in drawing Bollinger Bands, and because they are available on most, if not all, charting programs, you do not need to know any more than that about standard deviation in order to use the bands.

The bands are simply generated by the program drawing a 20-day simple moving average, which is the middle line. Bollinger experimented to find the best number of periods, and decided that 20 was the most effective to capture the variations in price. Then the upper and lower lines are drawn with lines at two standard deviations away from the middle line.

This means that the lines are following the average price, but also that the distance between the upper band and the lower band constantly varies, depending on the amount of fluctuation in price. The bands will draw closer together if the price is fairly stable, and spread out if it is swinging wildly. It is generally found that in a continuation, the range of prices is in an expanding band, whereas a band which compresses suggests that a reversal may happen soon. This is important information, as it suggests when a reversal may be likely, and that is what we usually try to capture with a candlestick pattern. In statistical terms, the two standard deviations used in the Bollinger Bands are supposed to capture 95 percent of the expected prices.

Charts with Bollinger Bands superimposed may appear magical. Frequently, when a stock is trending, the price will seem to walk up or walk down the band. In an uptrend, the candlesticks will often touch the upper band most of the way up. In fact, if they cease to be that close, then it is a sign that the trend may be ending. The opposite may also happen, and the price breaks out of the bands, indicating a change in sentiment toward the stock, but this is rarer.

Another sign of the failing of a trend is when the bands get closer to each other, as this shows a lack of movement in the price. The bands are a dynamic tool and well worth further study. You can find out more at **www. BollingerBands.com**.

Volatility

Bollinger Bands include volatility along with the trend and are therefore a tool combining these two aspects to provide traders with information. When you consider what tools you are going to use for technical analysis and trading based on that analysis, you need to be careful that you do not base confirmation on a different tool that has at its root in the same set of figures, as that does not give independent confirmation.

You may choose instead to gauge volatility from a separate indicator that quantifies the range of trading. For instance, the average trading range is just the average of the range from the low price to the high price for a number of days. Note that this includes the upper and lower shadows in the calculation of the range, taking the total swing each day as the important factor. This is a very basic indicator of how much a price is fluctuating.

There is a problem with it, though. If the price gaps from one day to the next, but each day trades in a small range, then the average trading range will be small, even though commonsense would say that the price is fluctuating significantly. This led Welles Wilder to invent an indicator called the Average True Range (ATR), which accounts for the gaps more realistically.

The ATR is simply calculated by using the range from one day's close to the next day's high, if the gap is upward. If the next day is bearish and gaps down, then the ATR is based on the range from the first day's close to the low of the second day. You can use the ATR and a moving average to set the range that you expect the stock to trade in and use it to identify potential breakouts. The use of this indicator makes evaluating the volatility more correct for trading purposes.

Fibonacci

Leonardo Fibonacci was an Italian who lived in the 12th and 13th centuries, and he has become known in the trading world for a set of ratios that derive from a series of numbers. He did not invent the series, as it was known in India at least seven centuries earlier, but in the same way that Steve Nison has brought the candlestick charting techniques to the Western world, Fibonacci brought the series to the attention of European mathematicians.

The number series leads to what is called the "Golden Ratio," or divine portion, which is numerically approximately 1.618 and known by the Greek letter phi (Φ). Pythagoras and Euclid both expounded on this number in their various works from pre-Christian times. The special feature of this number is that the inverse is exactly equal to the decimal portion — that is, in the region of 0.618. This is all that a trader needs to know, and even that is preprogrammed on charting software. If you have an interest in finding out more about it, the Web site **www.goldennumber.net** should more than satisfy your curiosity.

This ratio is the one that is understood to be the most pleasing to the human eye and mind, and is found in many places in nature, including spiders' webs and sunflower heads. The reason it is thought to have relevance in trading is that it conforms to the psychological expectations of fellow traders. In this task, it performs well, although it must be said that other ratios have been added to the golden ratio because they also were found to have trading significance. You will find 0.25, 0.382 (1-0.618), 0.5, 0.618, and 0.75 on many charting programs.

The ratio is used in two ways to try to identify targets and explain the resting places in the price chart. First, it is used in Fibonacci retracements, which are those occasions when an uptrend may decline for a short period. By stretching a Fibonacci overlay between the last major low point and the latest high, a series of lines corresponding to the Fibonacci values are drawn across the chart. When a price declines in the middle of an uptrend, it will often find support at one of the Fibonacci levels — typically, 0.618.

Fibonacci lines are also used to extend beyond the current price range in an effort to speculate where the new price target may be. In this case, you may be looking at a rally and a retracement that is reversing to start climbing upwards again. The Fibonacci lines are drawn from the latest low upward, with a size equal to the previous low-to-high range. Now each line becomes a possible target at which profits may be taken. As Fibonacci trading can be complex, with the ratios being used in many further ways, you should consult other references for more details and examples.

In our review of candlestick trading, the addition of Fibonacci lines to the price chart could be quite beneficial. When in either of those situations outlined above, the price approaches a Fibonacci level, we should examine the candlestick patterns carefully for any signs that might spell a reversal. Thus pre-warned, you should aim for maximum profits.

Mark Deaton, in his case study, talks of how he reviews Bollinger Bands and Fibonacci ratios for his stock selections.

CASE STUDY: MARK DEATON

mark@renegadetrader.com

www.candlestickgenius.com

What type of trading do you use candlesticks with — what markets and time periods?

I trade stocks with an emphasis on stock options. I use candlesticks and their patterns to help identify high probability zones. I trade a daily chart and five- to fifteen-minute charts.

When and how did you start getting interested in trading?

I don't exactly remember when I transitioned to candlesticks; I do, however, recollect that when I first began to study candlestick patterns, I immediately noticed that a high probability price pattern was instantly recognizable, whereas a bar chart price pattern required a little more looking at.

You could glance at a price chart with candlesticks and immediately recognize what price was doing. I found it to be extremely refreshing when looking at hundreds of charts a week.

CASE STUDY: MARK DEATON

Did you use candlestick charts from the start of your trading? If not, how much difference do you think they made to your trades when you learned to interpret them?

I started with a bar chart, and it was just too hard on the eyes. It's one thing to look at one chart and try and gauge price action; it's quite another to look at 100 charts.

Candlestick patterns provide more information; they are easily recognizable, and very easy on the eyes.

Do you enter a trade on the basis of a candlestick pattern only — always, sometimes, or never?

I can't say I have ever entered a trade based on a candlestick pattern only. I have exited trades based on only a doji at the top, on a long position, but never have I entered based only on a candlestick pattern.

I have entered based on a candlestick pattern and price action, meaning price was overextended to oversold on an uptrend and finding support at a key moving average. I've done that many times.

What other indicators do you use in conjunction with candlesticks if you want confirmation? Which do you find work best in combination with candle signals?

Bollinger Bands are an incredible partner to candlestick patterns. Whether you're a day trader or a swing trader, you can develop some incredible strategies with Bollinger Bands.

I also use Fibonacci retracements and extensions with candlestick patterns.

The three together are my magic formula (if there ever was one).

CASE STUDY: MARK DEATON

Do you use and find filters, such as price or volume, effective in assisting selection of worthwhile candlestick patterns?

Volume and price action are my main indicators, I rely on price action as the signal, I use my magic three above, and I use volume spikes as a tool for my trigger. Often, I will lay a 14- to 21-day SMA on volume and look for spikes in my direction as a trigger for entry.

There are many named candlestick patterns. Do you find that you only focus on a few, and if so, which?

I look at candlestick patterns generally without putting a name to them. Some I know so well I can't help it, but I have noticed that I can now read price action and gauge its current state while often not even seeing a particular pattern.

With that, I will often make trading decisions without a pattern present. For example, I might see two candlesticks at a bottom with long tails. A short real body with long tails tells me that the bears are trying awful hard to push price down, but by the close of the session, the bulls get price back up and close to the open.

This very often signifies that a bullish rally is imminent. A close look at volume is a perfect trigger here.

Is this just because you find them the most effective, or is it also because of other factors, such as how often they occur, for example?

This is simply because the underlying factors dictate that if price reaches way down but fails to stay there a couple of sessions in a row, its likened to a football team that keeps making it toward a touchdown but keeps getting pushed back to the 40-yard line.

After that happens a couple of times, it's just a matter of time before an interception.

● SAFETY ZONE ●

The goal of considering these oscillators and indicators is to identify trades with a high probability of going in the right direction and to determine in advance the risk/reward that each trade is expected to present. The next chapter, on trading psychology, introduces the idea of keeping a trading journal, and the information that you develop from these indicators should be recorded there so that you have a record from which you can learn.

If you do not learn from your bad trades, then you are doomed forever to repeat them. Make it a habit to print out a chart of the stock as you enter a position, note on the chart your observations that brought you to enter the trade, and insert or attach it in your journal at the appropriate page.

This will ensure that you think clearly and document your reasons in a way that can be understood, and if you are honest, it will provide you with valuable feedback on where you can improve.

Trading Psychology

Open any book on trading, and you will find a chapter about the psychology of trading. There have even been some trading books written that deal solely with the mental aspect of trading. Yet every year, beginning traders fail to understand or deal with the mental issues, and this is one of the major causes of their downfalls.

The Trading Plan

If you open an account and start trading without a defined plan, you may be lucky for a short time, but that will not last for long. You need to put a plan for trading in place, which will give you a way to trade consistently and a record that you can refer to so that you can refine any problems. Many traders recommend a plan that you can write down and could give to someone else to use. It would have all actions set out to cope with any contingency. I know that some successful traders claim that they eschew such formality and trade by the seat of their pants. I suspect that they have paid their dues over the years to become so experienced that they can recognize the trading opportunities from just looking.

I recommend that you prepare a trading plan before actually using your money for trading. The plan need not be complex; it could be something as easy as screening stocks for those where the RSI is less than 20 and buying those that develop a bullish engulfing pattern. You can position your stop-loss at twice the ATR away from the entry price, and add some Fibonacci lines to look for the profit targets.

Although many newcomers concentrate their attention on it, the entry only accounts for about 10 percent of your profits. Do not obsess about it; just make sure that the indications you are looking for are in place before making the trade. The entry to the trade is not finished until you set out your stop-loss position and your expected return, and note these in your trading journal. The following chapter on money management covers this topic in more detail.

The overriding reason that you need a trading plan at the start is that without comprehensive direction, you will be very vulnerable to trading from your gut and not with a clear head. As you experience the power of your emotions tugging at you when you trade, you will likely realize that would have been an unwise course.

As you develop your trading plan, you will need to back-test it against the markets you are going to trade. Again, although advisable, this may not be strictly necessary if you use common trading knowledge to craft the entry and exit points that you plan to use. It is important mentally, however, so that you can have faith in your plan and not question or alter it in an ad hoc manner when you are under pressure.

Beware of being a perfectionist. You are looking for consistency and a reasonable opportunity for profit. We all want to be right and not feel exposed to criticism, but you will never start to trade if your plan includes making sure that no trade can fail. Traders always seek the perfect entry, but you should concentrate more on money management, as that will make much more difference to your long-term trading prospects.

Sometimes, you will find that you missed the lowest point at which to buy; if the stock is still worth buying, then you should enter a position with no regrets, happy that it has already started moving in the correct direction and eased your immediate concern. At other times, you may hesitate to sell and wonder whether the pullback that follows will continue, or whether the rally will get back in its stride. If you have made a profit, you should consider the indications of the strength of the decline, and decide whether you would want to enter the position at that time. If not, then there is no good reason to stay in it.

An often overlooked strategy that you may consider is to average up. You may have heard of averaging down, which means to buy more stocks when the price goes down, on the basis that you are then paying less per stock on average, so any gains will be effectively larger when the price recovers. Sometimes, this is used for long-term investing, when the fundamentals are strong and the drop can be seen as a fluctuation. This strategy has no place in trading; in effect, you are just pouring good money after bad.

The opposite strategy is unexpectedly counterintuitive, but often a good choice. If you average up, it means that the stock has gone up, as you had hoped, and you buy more of it to profit from future growth. For some reason, this is difficult psychologically, even though it makes rational sense. The increase in price that you expected is already underway, and putting more money into the stock confirms the confidence that you had in your selection, which has already been shown to be a good one. There is just one proviso to this tactic — that you add together the total holding after averaging up, and make sure that it does not exceed a comfortable amount to have in a single company. The money management chapter following discusses your allocation guidelines and limits.

There will be times when you trade your plan and lose one trade after another. That is the nature of statistics, and if you change from a carefully considered plan to play a hunch when it happens, you will lose in the end. It is also in the nature of things that your hunch may work out, and this would reinforce your false impression that you have conquered the art and science of trading.

You should back-test and refine your trading plan until you are comfortable that, used consistently, it will give you the results that you want. Then, all you need is the discipline to stick with it in both good and bad times.

Fear and Greed

You may be surprised the first time you place a trade at how fearful you feel. Fear is perhaps the strongest of the emotions involved in trading, although greed can come in a close second. You may be afraid of many things, and if you cannot control yourself to overcome being scared, you may find that your new career becomes costly.

The most obvious fear is that you will lose all your money. As good as your trading plan may be, you will have some positions that lose, and the market will not follow its expected path. There is nothing that you can do about this, so you must learn to take it in stride. This challenge should be approached with careful money management and by adopting a certain play-money attitude to the funds, which hopefully are not supposed to be used for your next mortgage payment. This concept will be discussed in the next chapter.

Another fear involves your own perception of yourself and how you deal with what you may mistakenly think of as failure when a trade or several trades, do not work out as you had schemed and calculated. In your personal or business life, you may be used to making correct decisions and find it hard that it could be otherwise. For instance, if you are an engineer, you have a responsibility for the correct performance of what you design, and in some instances, such as structural engineering, the consequences of one mistake can be disastrous. If you recognize the issue, you will be halfway to solving it, even though the feeling of failure can initially be almost harder to bear than the actual loss.

You may fear that your friends and family will think less of you if you do not immediately have success with your trading. In fact, you may have mistakenly put yourself in that position by telling them how you were taking up a new hobby where you intended to make a fortune. While not keeping it a secret, it may be best not to talk too freely about trading until you have come to terms with what is required to do well.

Finally, you may fear that you are not up to the challenge of trading. This nurtures a feeling of inadequacy, which is not uncommon with people, particularly if you are from a troubled background where you have been challenged or told you will never make it. To overcome this, you must just prove them wrong by diligent application of the basics.

As for greed, no doubt you are trading with the intention of making some money if not getting rich. After all, there are other ways in which you can dispose of your assets, whether philanthropically or by gambling, and you might enjoy some of these more than sitting in front of a computer and trying to understand charts. Greed can creep up on you and affect your trading plan almost as easily as fear.

For instance, you may find that all the indicators you are following point to a reversal. This, you would assume, means that the trade is almost guaranteed to succeed. You wait for and get a candlestick reversal pattern to show that the time is right, and your only hesitation on entering a position is whether you should double up on your calculated stake to help buy that new monitor you need to make your trading career easier. Greed overcomes you, and you put in too much, only to find that the hot stock was not listening to the indicators and went the wrong way.

Now, do you close your position and sell for a loss, knowing that some trades will lose, or do you curse that you put in so much that you cannot afford for the trade to fail, still convinced that the indications are good, and it is only a blip before the inevitable rise and profit making? Now fear takes over control of your actions. This is how fear and greed conspire to make you regret ever trying trading in the first place.

You may have noticed that greed was almost as bad as fear. One point you should note about trading is that markets tend to rise more slowly than they fall. Once they start going down, the loss of value can be quite rapid. Generally speaking, the bull market is driven by greed. The price rises as more people buy and want to make some money from the stock, which they see is on the rise. This continues until the stock is overbought and ready to reverse.

On the other hand, the fall in the price of the bear market becomes driven by fear, particularly as traders see the losses start to build. Market participants, at least those that have long positions, or own the stock, scurry to unload the shares as fast as their fingers can take them, and this contributes to the collapsing prices that we observe from time to time, such as recently in 2008. So fear is the dominant force, with greed coming in second place.

The good news is that you are not alone in facing these emotions. All traders have them and only some overcome them by using persistence, discipline, and courage. Many traders give up, and the statistics say that 90 percent of beginners fail in the first six months of trying to take up trading. Everyone has a deeply personal battle to control their emotions when trading. To be in trading for the long-term, you must learn a level of self control and discipline that you may not have experienced before.

Other Emotions

When trading, you will run the gamut of emotions, and the way you react and deal with them is key to your success. Performers and public speakers often say that their emotions and nerves before a show are natural and can be harnessed to enhance their performance. They have learned to acknowledge their fears and feed off them to give an edge to what they do and help them excel. The same cannot be said of trading. Almost without exception, any emotion can stand in your way of a consistent trading performance.

Hope is to be left out of the equation, as the market is not in tune with your needs or wishes and will ruthlessly go its own way, regardless of your feelings. What you need to cultivate is a dispassionate attitude that only requires you to think "Oh, well" if a trade goes bad, and then steps back to let you make the next trade.

You will need to cultivate confidence in order to trade your plan effectively. Confidence that you can trade and profit will only come with trading education and positive results. The lack of confidence can lead to many self-defeating practices; for instance, you may hesitate to act on your plan when times get tough if you are not confident that you are capable of trading and have made a good plan.

You can work on aspects of your confidence in various ways. For one, you will develop confidence in your plan and be more inclined to stick with it if you have adequately paper traded it before going live. You do not need to become arrogant in your knowledge and abilities — indeed, in time, the market will teach you a lesson if you do — but you should cultivate a quiet assurance that you can do what is necessary to trade profitably.

Another attribute that you need to work on may be patience. This comes into trading in two ways. First, you need patience to hold on to your cash and not put it in a half-likely trade just because you have not made a pick all week. Also, you should try not to be a perfectionist and wait for the perfect moment before trading, but instead there is a happy medium that you should strive for. Your money does not need to be in the market if there is not an appropriate place for it to be, and you do not need to compromise your trading plan just to facilitate a trade. Your money is never safer than when it is cash in your account, and your priority, as you will discover in the next chapter, is to protect what you have.

You also need to exercise patience when you are in a successful trade. There is a saying, "cut your losses and let your profits run," and both halves of the saying are significant. You should never hesitate to cut your losses if the trade turns against you, and on the other hand, you may need patience to let your profits run and wait until the best return is made. The instinct is to take your profit quickly from a winning trade so that it is "in the bank," and this is accompanied by a good feeling. For best returns, you may need to watch it go up for several days, even if in smaller steps, and not rush to close out your position.

Trading Journal

One tool that is used by many successful traders is the trading journal or trading diary. With this, you have a multi-faceted tool to help you get better at many aspects of trading. Opinions vary on the best format for a journal, as some say that as you are trading at a computer, you should use word processing or diary software. I think that a physical journal, preferably of some quality, enhances the respect that you pay to the duty of recording your day, and increases its worth to you.

The journal must include each trade that you make as a matter of record. It should also contain much more. The basic inclusion would be a note of the trade, including name, date, time, and amount, with a printout of the chart and handwritten notes about the entry point and the way in which this satisfied your plan criteria. Subsequently, you would track the stock, and finally, make an entry when it was disposed of, stating for what reason and for how much. I recommend a sticky note attached to the edge of each page where the trade is still in progress so that you can turn to it easily.

In addition to this hard information, your journal can be used to track your feelings on each event and provide valuable feedback on where your emotions have affected your decisions. A journal is a useless document, except perhaps for you at tax preparation time, unless you take time to review it and determine where your trading is going right and where it is going wrong.

You might find that you consistently overtrade on a certain configuration, and that it does not work out over time, causing you to refine your trading plan. You may also see that you second guess your plan when certain circumstances happen; if the results are good, you might want to change your plan, but it is more likely that you will be able to see this as a weakness that you need to concentrate on improving.

Above all, you should examine your entries on your feelings and see how you are coping with the stresses of trading and where you may need help. To read these entries in retrospect can help in maintaining your perspective and focus on the task at hand.

Although, you should not attempt to review your trades on the same day that you took them, particularly if they were losers; there will be too much emotion bound up in the business for you to make a dispassionate assessment. You will discover for yourself the amount of time you need to let pass before review, and it should allow you to approach the evaluation in a detached way, as if you were looking at someone else's journal, when you can make a cool judgment on any matters that require you to change your *modus operandi*.

● SAFETY ZONE ●

It always seems to surprise people that success in a career that seems so mathematical and analytical is actually so heavily influenced by emotion. You may have been drawn to trading by an interest in calculations and numbers and such an aptitude will not be wasted. You will also need to deal with aspects of your thinking outside this controlled and regulated area, and it is how well you can exercise your willpower that may decide your future profits.

Do not underestimate the impact that trading with real money can have on your psyche. Until you have tried it, you will probably be confident that you are able to control yourself in any situation, but the truth will prove to be different, if you are like most people.

Recording your feelings in your trading journal will let you come back later to review and rationalize them, and can help your progress to the efficient trader that you seek to become.

Money Management

Along with the mental approach, money management is a crucial aspect of trading. You may be surprised to hear that the main goal of trading is to preserve your trading capital. If you lose all your money, then the game is over, so you must do all you can to not lose your money.

Many newcomers to trading think that its primary purpose should be to make money, but if you concentrate on not losing what you have, making money happens much more easily and quickly. It is a way of adjusting your attitude to the exploit that will make it more profitable and ensuring that you are not forced to give up your ambition to be a trader prematurely by lack of funds.

Placing Your Trade

With the Internet, anyone who wants to do so can trade without ever seeing or talking to a broker. You can place trades more easily online than through the telephone, and there are many discount brokers where you can trade for less than $10. A simple search will bring you more offers than you need, and you should get an account set up with one of the major brokers.

There are still brokers available that will give you the full service, including stock picks and alerts, but you need not use these when you are trading on your own account and making your selections. These brokers have a place with long-term investors who need the assistance, but are not suited to short-term trading.

If you have not explored the offered facilities, you may be surprised at just how much information is readily available at no additional cost. Even the cheapest online broker will give you access to customizable charts for every stock offered, and these tools are more than adequate for starting your trading career. Free Web sites, such as Yahoo!®, often delay the stock prices for a period of 20 minutes and do not give streaming quotes, but these services are adequate for many traders, particularly those who use the daily charts and just enter their trades each day in the evening. You will even find automatic candle pattern detection, which allow you to zero in quickly on the stocks of interest to you. **Stockcharts.com**, whose stock charts are used in this book, has such a facility at no charge, with additional features for a small subscription. **HotCandlesticks.com** is another company that specializes in identifying candlestick patterns to assist your trading.

When you want to place a trade, you will sign in to your brokerage account and simply enter the code for the stock and the number of shares required and select the type of order. Other markets have a similar, straightforward process.

You have a choice on the way in which your order is processed. The simplest is to use a market order, which buys the stock at the price prevailing when your order is processed by the broker. This guarantees that you get the stock, although it may be at a slightly different price from what you saw last on the Web site. You may run into this, particularly if the stock is thinly traded, when there are likely to be bigger fluctuations in the price.

The actual trading process is highly automated and usually happens quickly after you have placed your order.

Another choice of order type is the limit order, which is a way of guaranteeing the price but not the execution. With the limit order, you specify the price you want to pay or how much you want to sell a holding for, and the broker will process the transaction if they can get that price or better. If you suspect that a stock price is moving quickly, and you only want to buy it if you can get it for a certain price, then you would use the limit order. If the price moves too quickly, you will not get the shares, but that was the decision that you made by placing a limit order. Be warned that the order will be in effect for the period you specified, so if the order did not get filled immediately, you may find that the price dips later in the day, and you are committed to buying the stocks, even if you decided in the meantime to buy something else. It is best to cancel an unfulfilled limit order to avoid any confusion.

A third way to buy or sell shares is with a stop order, which allows you to control when a market order is executed. Typically seen as a stop-loss order, the order will be triggered when the price reaches a certain level. For the sell stop order, you would set a price below the current price, and if the price dropped that low, the stock would be sold. This provides some protection from losing too much if the price goes against you, which is why it is called a stop-loss. Note that you may not get the amount that you selected, as the order becomes a simple market sell order once triggered by the price movement; if the price has gapped down, it may be less than you set, and the sale would still take effect.

Although this is the most familiar use of the stop order, it can also be used to buy shares subject to reaching a triggering level. In this case, the stop price is set above the current price. If the price increases to that level, then the order becomes a market buy order and is executed. This means that you do not buy the shares unless they are going up in value.

The stop-limit order is a useful variant of the order types. The stop-limit becomes a limit order when the stop price is reached — you can set a different stop price and limit price. This has the caveat that, as a limit order, your order may not be filled even if triggered, depending on the price movement. This type of order is sometimes used by traders if they are expecting a breakout of, for example, the Squeeze Alert pattern — a reducing triangular formation — and want to cover their trade in either direction. You would set up two trades — one to buy if the stock went above a certain level, which would then be the stop level, and the other to sell short if the price went below another stop level.

This brings us to the idea of selling short. Although for some, the concept of selling what you do not own seems confusing, the broker takes care of the details. There are some possible problems, which are to do with the availability of shares and paying any dividends due out of your account, but as a rule, the system works well. When you place an order to sell short, you are asking the broker to sell borrowed shares for you, and you anticipate that they will lose value so that you can replace them later by buying at a lower price, yielding a profit to you.

The final type of order we will review here is the trailing stop order. This is an order that is used to protect your profit automatically. It is used when your stock is increasing in price, and you want to ensure that you do not allow the gains to vanish on a downtrend. With this order, you set an amount, as either a percentage or a value, which you will allow the price to drop by before you want your shares to be sold. The trailing stop order tracks up behind the share price, automatically adjusting, and the sell order will take place when the price falls and the amount below the peak is reached. Thus, you do not have to be watching your shares continually, and you will only chance losing a small part of your gains.

If you need further details on these types of orders and on others that are available, you should contact your broker.

Trading Funds

Because of the stress of trading, it is essential that you only trade with money that you will accept losing. You must be financially secure and able to make your mortgage and car payments without relying on the money in your trading account. This concept ties back into the chapter on psychology; if you are trading with money that you cannot give up, you will be a scared trader and will likely be severely tempted to be irrational, if not desperate, in your trades.

You may have heard that you should paper trade before risking real money — that is, pretend that you are trading and write down your trades, keeping a running total of your gains and losses. This is a good idea, although it usually does not give you any inkling of the fear you will experience with real trading using real money. However, if you can manage it, the way you feel when paper trading is exactly the attitude that you want when you approach your real trading. In that way, you will not feel emotionally attached to the dollar-by-dollar account balance and will be able to trade rationally and in accordance with your plan.

When you start trading, you will need to set aside the funds that you are going to be using, and then treat them as if they were no longer yours. How would you feel if you had several losing trades, and your initial funds were reduced by 25 or 50 percent? Would you be inclined to give up trading? If so, perhaps those funds were not really available for your trading in the first place, at least in your mind.

When you are in a trade, you need to focus on keeping hold of all the money that you can and protecting any profits that you make. This means two things. If the trade goes down to your predetermined stop-loss level, you should exit and move on. If you think it is hard (and it is when you start) to close a trade where you lose 10 percent of the money that you paid, you should think about the possible consequences of not doing so.

You may be forced with closing the trade and taking 20 percent or even 50 percent losses, and that is difficult to do.

On the other hand, if you enter a trade, and it does go the right way, you should be sure to raise your stop-loss level, whether on the market or just in your notes, to protect what you have made. With the one proviso that you should not make it so close to the price that the market fluctuations will see you stopped out prematurely, this is an important discipline that will lead to success. If the price goes up as you expect, and then declines back to the start because you did not take your profits, you again will find it difficult to close the trade. If the decline continues, a winning pick might become a loser, and you will find that hurts even more than a pick that loses from the start.

Approach to Allocation

Having settled on some "play money" for your trading account, you will need to consider the level of risk that you will assume. Given that you are detached from the emotional aspect of losing this money, you still need to stay in the game if you want to trade, and capital preservation is the principal objective.

Below is a table of how much you have to earn to make up losses.

AMOUNT LOST	AMOUNT NEEDED TO RECOVER TRADING CAPITAL
10%	11%
20%	25%
30%	43%
40%	67%
50%	100%
60%	150%

As you can see, it is much easier to lose money than to make it back. If you were to risk 10 percent of your money on each trade, and you had a run of five losses, which is not unlikely if you trade for a while, then you would lose 50 percent, but you would have to earn 100 percent on the money remaining in order to re-establish your original capital.

While there are many combinations of numbers of consecutive losing trades, such as how likely they are and the amount risked, a widely used figure for an acceptable risk of loss is 2 percent, with a maximum of 20 percent in any particular trade. You will find some variations from these figures, and the final choice is yours, but they work for many people.

The 2 percent loss may sound very small, but you must consider it in context. Successive losing trades will occur, should you be trading for any length of time, and this level of loss allows you a reasonable course for recovery. You should apply this percentage to your current account and not keep using the initial figure calculated from your opening balance.

The 2 percent represents the amount that you can lose on a trade, and this may require some calculation. You will need to take into account where your stop-loss point is, should the trade run against you, and work out how much money you can afford to trade on this basis. Then, ensure that no more than 20 percent of your money will be involved if you trade based on this calculation and adjust your ideas for the trade if necessary.

If you are trading derivatives, such as options or futures, then you will be involved with different calculations from those related to stock trading. For instance, with options, you have a chance of losing all the money you use to buy the option, if the option finishes out of the money at the strike date. The calculating back of the 2 percent limit is thus very simple — it is just your cost for the option, which you stand to lose entirely — and this can limit your exposure. You should not change your limits to suit your whims, as a number of consecutive losing trades on options, which can surely happen, would hamper your trading career just as surely as losing 2 percent on going long on stocks would. With futures, you will need to assess a realistic exposure and work out from there the size of contract that you can afford.

Making Your Picks

Many books, articles, and courses have been and are being written about stock selection. The fundamentals do not change, but the way they are packaged may be renewed with every new release. The information in this book is extensive regarding candlestick patterns and indicative on other factors and indicators, as those are not the purpose of this book. If you are particularly interested in another aspect of trading, then I would advise you to seek out more information to help you plan out your trading and write your trading plan. Some references that I have experience on are listed in the resources section of this book, but the list is by no means comprehensive.

You may start with a specific trading plan from some source, but if you want to stay ahead of the trend and the bulk of the traders, you will find that you need to personalize the plan and update it at intervals. Consider this — if a published plan was to be the perfect plan, which we would have to define as a plan that provided a minimum number of losses and/or a maximum return on the successful trades as no plan can avoid occasional losses, then as a result of its widespread availability, it would cease to be perfect. It would cause its own failure, as the action of many traders using it would change the results.

This is not as depressing as it might sound, as developing your own plan includes incorporating your own style and risk tolerance and can be recommended as a good learning exercise. The secret is to start with clear, established guidelines and see how they work together, for this is all that a successful plan uses. I have given some indication about the factors to take into account when considering your trading plan.

You should explore at least the well known indicators to see which you feel you can understand, as a black box indicator is to be shunned. For a cautious approach, an expansion of the plan would be to find a second indicator that is not based on the same fundamentals as the first — this is important, as two indicators based on the same information are likely to point in the same way, regardless of whether it is correct in this case.

When considering your plan, you should bear in mind that a whole range of market indication is available from various moving average combinations, which can be used for proving trends as well as giving crossover signals. You are not restricted to the messages from calculated oscillators.

Whether you decide to use one or two factors indicating that there is pressure for a reversal, you would need to paper trade in your selected market and establish your confidence in the plan, refining your indicators and experimenting with different ones as needed. It is important to note that the success of your plan is not measured by how many trades go the right way compared with the number that do not. Success is maximizing the trading profit potential, which includes the amount of money lost or gained on each trade.

While there is software for candlestick pattern recognition, you can also simply print out a historical chart, including your indicators, scan for indication of the correct condition that you would seek, such as oversold and hooking back, and then view the candlestick patterns day by day to see when you would have initiated a trade and the result. Such hands-on review can give you further insight into the factors that affect your profit.

Figuring Your Stops

Much has been written about the risk/reward ratio when trading, and many people have a rule of thumb that the expected reward or gain should be two or three times the perceived risk or loss. I would postulate that this only addresses a part of the picture and that the trader who wants to make safe returns would do well to consider a wider context.

I suggest that the probability of a trade succeeding should also be considered in selecting the optimum strategy. Perhaps the trades that offer a 1 to 3 risk/reward ratio only move in the right direction two-thirds of the time, and other trades with a 1 to 2 risk/reward ratio succeed more than 90 percent of the time. With the first—30 average tradest—you would gain 60 units and lose 10; with the second, you would gain 54 units and lose 3. The latter would offer a slightly better prospect, in addition to being more psychologically acceptable. This is yet another factor to figure into your trading. In fact, it is easy to construct a situation where your trades go into profit less than half the time, but you still make more money than with trades that succeed much more often.

The risk is associated with where your initial stop loss is positioned, and there are a number of ways to set this. The stop loss is the Plan B of a trade — if Plan A does not work, and the stock does not move in the desired direction, then Plan B takes effect and takes you out of the trade for a small loss. You should never enter a trade without considering your stop-loss position, although whether you actually place it in the market depends on whose advice you follow and what markets you are trading in. If you are day trading and have a "Level II" screen, you will be familiar with how you can see potential orders at different prices lined up on display; some experts believe that markets are manipulated to capture your stocks with a quick dip in value if your stop is placed on the market and is therefore public knowledge.

The overriding idea of a stop loss is to prevent you from losing more than is necessary if the trade is wrong. If it is too close to the existing price, then simple market fluctuations may cause the price to dip before taking off. To adhere to your trading plan would require that you sell at a loss, when the pick was actually sound and subsequently, would have made money. If this happens too often, you might be tempted on the next occasion to deviate from your plan, and that is never recommended. On the other hand, a stop loss that is too far away would allow you to lose more than you should need to on a losing trade.

The stop loss is an intrinsic part of your trading plan or system, and it is used when back checking the performance. When you are using candlesticks as part of your plan, the stop loss may be associated with the length of the previous shadow in the undesirable direction plus an arbitrary margin, with the reasoning that if it is reached, the reversal has not happened as expected.

Another system of setting the stop loss, favored for its simplicity, is to decide on a certain amount or percentage that the stop loss will be from the entry price. While this is easy to understand, it is an arbitrary method that is likely to be non-optimal. If you look at different charts, you can see that some stocks have quite dissimilar daily ranges, so you may find that stops set in this way are too small for some and too large for others.

If you are trading near a support or resistance that you have already determined, you can set your stop on the basis that the price should not do more than approach the line, and not pass through it. Strictly speaking, there is a chance that a support or resistance is briefly penetrated and still holds its value; there are no absolutes in trading. You would compensate for this by setting your stop slightly outside the bounds that you have established. This method of selecting the stop-loss position can be fairly effective, as it is related to the actual stock performance shown in the chart.

Finally, another stop-loss technique that is related to the actual stock performance is one based on the average true range (ATR) of a stock. This calculated measure of a stock's volatility is available on most charting packages. It derives from the true range of fluctuation in the price, which is averaged for a period of time, often 14 days, in order to smooth out the value. To use it for a stop-loss, you could set the stop a multiple of the ATR value away from your buying price, as this would allow the stock room to vary normally, while triggering if there was a move that was larger compared with the normal variations.

The other side to the risk/reward calculation is the potential reward for the trade you are contemplating. There are many factors that can be taken into account for this assessment, and the choice of method depends on some extent what sort of trading you are involved with. With some trading techniques, you will have determined the current support and resistance levels, and you are contemplating that the share price will retrace to these lines or to an intermediate position that is based on the Fibonacci ratios and lines. The use of Fibonacci levels was touched on briefly in Chapter 14 and much has been written about the supposed properties of these lines. Whether because of other traders' expectations or because of some natural law, the argument is that traders tend to use these ratios as critical turning points, and thus, they can represent price targets.

Fibonacci is also referenced on a breakout, when the ratios are extended beyond the previous high and low range to project how far the price may go before a consolidation. Advocates claim that the Fibonacci ratios are predictive, and this may become a self-fulfilling prophecy. Regardless of the reason, these ratios have been shown to be accurate quite often in determining resting or turning points in the price chart and represent reasonable expectations of the targets.

While on the subject of stops, you should not forget to adjust your stops to protect your profits as the share price rises. These can be trailing stops on the market, subject to the reservations expressed earlier about putting your stops on the market, or they can be stops that you have a note of in your trading journal. To protect your gains is one of the most important factors, as a volatile stock will often retrace, and you do not want to lose all of your gains by not protecting them.

The level of the stop can be calculated in a similar manner to the stop loss. It may be the current price less a certain percentage or amount. The important point is that this stop ratchets up — that is, it never comes back down. If the price comes down to meet it, then the stop is triggered, and the stock is sold. You can also use a multiple of the ATR as the margin before the stop is triggered.

● **SAFETY ZONE** ●

Before you spend one cent from your trading account, you should practice until you are sure of your plan and your ability to follow it. This is called paper trading, and it is the same as actually trading, but without spending any money. You must treat it as seriously as if you were using real money, and this you may find a challenge at first.

When you paper trade, you write down in your trading journal your intentions and your reasons for the trade, and keep score of the hypothetical expenditure, being sure to include broker commissions and using the prices online at the time of your decisions. Your broker in practice might improve these, as he has a duty of "best execution," but it is not wise to assume so. It is hard to regard paper trading in the same way as trading with actual money, but it is the best option available to prepare you for the action to come. Bear in mind that if you do not manage to generate some feeling of reality when you paper trade, the transition to a live account will be that much more difficult.

As you feel confident enough to try real trading, bear in mind that your goal is to preserve your capital. If your trades are good, the profit will take care of itself; but if you do not preserve your funds, your trading career will be curtailed. When you do have to take a loss, just mentally shrug your shoulders and then put the thought behind you. Once you have dismissed it from worrying you, then you can go back to your journal and see whether you could have done anything differently — and sometimes you cannot.

Other Charting Methods

The preceding chapters have detailed the way that candlesticks have been adopted into general use in the West. It is interesting to look at some variations that are not so well known, for which Steve Nison is also responsible, and see what advantages can be realized from taking a different view.

Sakata's Method

Sakata's Method is, strictly speaking, not very different from the way that Western candlestick charting has been adopted. Sakata was the name of the port in Japan where Homma ran his business in the 18th century. It is still an important port, and in those days, it was a major rice trading center. Sakata's Method is understood to be the system that Homma himself invented and used. It is based around the number three, and some aspects of it you have already encountered — for instance, in the Three White Soldiers pattern and in the Three Crows patterns.

The basic principles used in Sakata's Method include some that you will readily recognize from modern theory. For instance, it is stated that prices will continue to move in an established direction, whether trending up or down, which expresses the idea of momentum in a market. It is also harder for a market to rise than it is for it to lose value; the traditional saying with that concept is that a market can fall under its own weight.

Another two truisms expounded under Homma's philosophy are that every trend will change in time, and that sometimes, there will not be a discernible trend. The first means that markets do not keep going up endlessly, but sometimes come down, and that a bear market will become bullish after a while. When trading, it is possible to overlook this simple idea when the times are good and believe that the only way is up; but the depression of 2008 provides a recent reminder that all good things must come to an end. The second point acknowledges that markets are not always trending, but sometimes go sideways, or without any appreciable movement up or down. In fact, this happens more often than most people realize, and it requires a different approach to trading or even staying out of that market altogether.

Three Gaps

The Japanese name for Three Gaps is *San-Ku*, *San* meaning "three" and *Ku* meaning "gap," and it is an example of the thought that all good things must come to an end. When there are three gaps in the price chart, Homma's way is to sell out of the trade on the third gap, and this applies whether you are trading long — that is, buying the stock in an uptrend — or trading short, in a downtrend.

The sentiment that this idea encapsulates is that the first gap is the result of great enthusiasm and little doubt that the trend will continue. The second gap represents additional buying by those who are catching up with the trend. By the time the third gap happens, the trading is taking place on behalf of the slower market watchers, and the trend may be losing steam. That is why Sakata's Method recommends selling on the third gap, before the overbought conditions are realized, and the selling begins.

This philosophy is expressed in the Three Gaps Up pattern described earlier. A similar argument is advanced for a bear movement, and this leads to the Three Gaps Down pattern.

Three Methods

The principle of the three methods is embodied in the continuation patterns of the Rising Three Method and the Falling Three Method. The thought behind these is that the market needs to take a rest, or pause, sometimes in a trend. The fact is that trends often do not continue uniformly without a break or consolidation. This does not mean that the trend has ceased, and the three methods are continuation patterns that take a period of rest into account.

Three Mountains

Homma's work included considering the overall patterns that the stock charts can make, and the Three Mountains pattern is an example of an observation that he made that has an equivalent in Western charting techniques. If you have knowledge of Western charting methods, you may be familiar with the "triple top" and the "head and shoulders." The Three Mountains is a similar pattern.

The Three Mountains, *San-Zan*, shows a top in the market. The price chart rises and falls three times, and the resulting triple peak is counted as showing a top in the price. In this case, the tops are at approximately the same height or may slope slightly downward. The head-and-shoulders is a similar Western pattern, and as the name suggests, the center peak is slightly higher.

Three Rivers

This pattern, called *San-Sen* in Japanese, occurs in various references in different ways, so the exact intention of Homma is not clear. The most obvious interpretation is that this is the opposite of the Three Mountains, and equivalent to the triple bottom of Western classic trading theory. An alternative meaning is the use of three candlesticks to indicate a bullish reversal, and you can see this in the Unique Three River Bottom.

The use of three lines to signal a bullish reversal is not restricted to this pattern; for instance, the Morning Star is sometimes called the Three Rivers Morning Star. To further confuse matters, the same phrase has been used to describe top reversal patterns, such as Three Rivers Upside Gap Two Crows, which is a bearish reversal described previously. This leads to some conjecture that the term Three Rivers refers simply to patterns that signal on the basis of three candlesticks.

Three Soldiers

The Japanese term *San-Pei* literally means "three soldiers marching in the same direction," and while this is exemplified by the three-day candlestick pattern Three White Soldiers, the three soldiers that Homma referred to covered many more of the patterns discussed, such as Deliberation and Advance Block. In fact, the Three Soldiers category applies to any pattern where the three candlesticks are consistently moving in the same direction, which means that Three Black Crows and Identical Three Crows are also considered to be part of the family of the Three Soldiers formation.

While Sakata's method focuses on the number three in the ways described above, it also involves the consideration of larger formations that give an overall shape to the price chart. Some of these have equivalent ideas in the traditional Western technical analysis, and the use of candlesticks can give a new perspective.

High Waves

Particularly noticeable when using candlestick charting, the concept of the High Wave formation is that there are a series of candles with long upper shadows following from an uptrend. From the method of drawing the candlesticks, you can see that this represents a number of days where the highest price at which the security traded has been well above the opening and closing prices.

In specific candlestick terms, this may be represented individually as a Shooting Star, a Gravestone Doji, or a Spinning Top, all bearish reversal signs. The formation may even include an Advance Block pattern. When you see several of these together, this makes a High Waves pattern. The psychology of this is plain, and the collection of several of these candlesticks into the pattern serves to emphasize their message of change.

The long upper shadows that fail to hold into the close of the session clearly show that there is a loss of direction in the market, and the bulls are unable to keep pushing the price up. The natural consequence is that this is a turning point, and the price will decline.

Eight New Price Lines

Eight New Price Lines is a formation that consists of a succession of higher prices. You may be able to guess the meaning of this from some of the previous commentary. The formation of eight new highs in the price, or in some references, ten or twelve new highs, has an implication that the market will be getting tired, and it may be a good time to take profits before a reversal. In some ways, you may think that this is against the old trading adage of "cutting your losses, and letting your profits run," and whether it is good advice depends on the particular circumstances.

As with many of these inferences and meanings, there is no sure thing in the market, and you should judge the value of this formation suggesting a reversal by looking at other indicators and oscillators to see whether they concur. At the least, it may give you a reason to review your stop, and make sure that your trailing stop is protecting your profits from too much of a loss if the reversal happens.

Tweezers

The tweezers concept was introduced in Chapter 7, where it was presented as two candlesticks with identical high or low prices, which may mark a position of resistance or support when in a trend. The more general application of this includes any number of periods but with the two candles on either side, sandwiching other candles that do not breach the level. You can see a similar concept in the Stick Sandwich patterns and in the Matching patterns.

As candlesticks for the most part do not provide assistance in determining levels, this formation is a valuable one to note. If subsequently, other candles touch the same level but do not pass through it, the level is considered more strongly indicated, and this is called confirmation.

Tower Tops and Tower Bottoms

Another multi-candle formation, the Tower Top and Tower Bottom are named for the number of long candles that are present. The Tower Top, in a rising market, is started with a number of long white candles that may get gradually shorter, with some changing color. The price stops making highs and a flat top in the chart. As time passes, the passing of the top is finally marked by a long black day, marking the start of the decline. The Tower Top, although mainly long candles, can also have the occasional short candlestick during this transition of the colors. Eventually, you would expect the candles to become more predominantly black and set new lows as the market reverses and declines.

The Tower Bottom is the opposite, as you might expect, consisting of long black days that give way to long white days and start to rally. Again, the occasional short candlestick during the finding of the bottom does not detract from the validity of the formation. The long white day that marks the end of the bottom preferably has a good volume to show that it is a firm reversal of the trend.

Fry Pan Bottom

In contrast to the Tower Bottom, the Fry Pan Bottom is a similar shape but has all short days. The formation is a rounded bottom after a decline, and the colors of the candlesticks are not important.

The feature of this formation is that after a number of days forming a bottom, the price takes off with a gap up to a bullish white day, and this should mark the beginning of the expected rally. The formation is similar to the cross-section of a frying pan, which is where the name derives. You should find that the volume reduces in the middle of the formation, and then it picks up when the price jumps to complete the pattern and rally the price.

Dumpling Top

The opposite of the Fry Pan Bottom, the Dumpling Top is the short-bodied version of the Tower Top. In an uptrend, the rate of price increase slows and forms a dome with short-bodied candles of either color. The Dumpling Top reversal is completed when there is a gap down to a black-bodied candle, and the decline begins. Even though this is a decline, typically, you would expect that the volume is lowest in the middle of the top and increases to clearly mark the downtrend that is starting.

High Price Gapping Play

The High Price Gapping Play is what the Western trader would recognize as a breakout through the resistance level. Sometimes, the price will consolidate around a certain range for a time, and the High Price Gapping Play is defined as the movement of the price upward, which breaks through the established range. This price movement includes a gap from the previous day, which is a sign of strength and an unleashing of the buying pressure that has been restrained by the range.

Low Price Gapping Play

The complementary formation to the High Price Gapping Play is the Low Price Gapping Play, and this is the opposite of the previous description. Again, the price gets stuck in a range and continually tests the support level, which confirms it temporarily. Eventually, the bearish pressure overcomes the support, and the price gaps downward to a bearish candlestick, which points to the decline that is to come.

Three-Line Break

The three-line break is a way of looking at candlestick charting that discerns the trends reliably. This can give a signal for trading entries and exits, although some say that it is often late. The method depends on the idea that a trend has momentum and continues until a reversal is forced on it, as set out in Sakata's Method above.

The system of plotting the three-line break is defined and unambiguous, and thus, systematically shows the trend. First, it should be noted that the three-line break system only uses one price per period, and that is, by definition, the closing price.

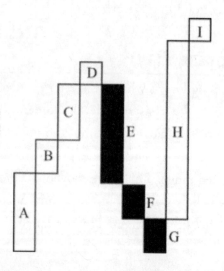

Three-Line Break Example

If you commence, say, with an uptrend, the first line will be white, based on the closing price yesterday up to the closing price for today. This is drawn as a white rectangle, A , in the figure. The closing price for each day following is noted, but nothing is plotted unless the price finishes above the closing price already plotted at the top, when a new white line, or rectangle, is drawn from the existing line to the new level, as shown at point B.

Again, closing prices are ignored for the next days until the closing price exceeds the last high for B. When it does, the next line, C, is drawn from the last to the new high.

You will note that this system means that the horizontal axis is not drawn to scale for time — for instance, A may last for two days before B is drawn, B may encompass two weeks before C is drawn, and C may only be a day before being passed. The plot gives no scale to this, although the actual days may be denoted along the bottom for reference.

The idea is that you only plot a new line when you have a reason to — that is, when it makes a new high.

In explaining this simply, I have purposely ignored the possibility that the price may go down and assumed a simple uptrend so that you can understand the concept. However, obviously, in the real world, the closing price can go down too, and I have shown a downtrend with black lines in the diagram. The change between an uptrend and a downtrend is triggered by the closing price falling below the low of the third previous line, which is where the name three-line break derives.

Look again at the figure. After the uptrend makes a new line at D, no higher closing prices are made, and the price starts to decline. The closing prices on subsequent days could be anywhere in the range from the bottom of B to the top of D, and nothing would be drawn, perhaps for weeks. When the price drops so low that it is less than the low of B, which is the third line, the black bearish line E is drawn as shown.

Now that the chart is on a downtrend, new black lines are drawn whenever a new low is made, hence making F and G. I have shown another reversal here, where the price stopped making new lows and started rallying. Until there is a new low, or the price goes higher than the third line back, which is labeled E, there will again be no lines drawn on the chart.

On the day represented by the line H, the closing price was higher than the top of E, so the reversal was confirmed and a white bullish line drawn, starting another uptrend. Each time a line is drawn that changes the color, such as this one, it is called a turnaround day.

Consider what this method achieves. The need for a price to exceed that of the third previous line for a reversal means that it has to be of a certain size in order to be drawn, so the method makes sure that small and insignificant reversals that do not amount to much are filtered out and never seen or traded.

The three-line break can be traded by taking a position when there is a turnaround day, which would mean buying the stock on the day after H was plotted, for instance. The stock would be sold on the next turnaround, when the white lines changed back to black. A stop loss would be placed at the low level of H, to sell at a loss if the stock price moved against your expectation. Now, you may see that this has the possibility of not being a good system. Considering the length of H, which it had to be in order to trigger the turnaround, there may be an amount of money left on the table before the method signals a buy, even when it is a winning trade. The other point to note is that the system fails when there is no clear trend, and the stock is drifting sideways.

The three-line break can also be used as an overbought or oversold indicator. For this, you would just count the number of consecutive white or black lines, and if there were ten or more, you might decide that the price had run its course and was due for a reversal.

As with all indicators, it is prudent to have a different one to confirm or deny the trade. The three-line break can be used with conventional candlestick charting or with any other technical indicators.

The three-line break is available, just as candlestick charts are, in many charting packages, and here is a comparison between a conventional candlestick chart and a three-line break chart for the same stock.

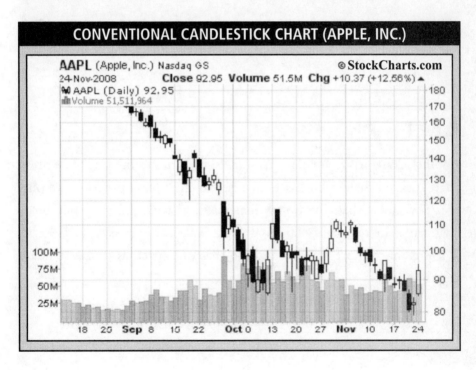

Notice how the three-line chart hides the detail of the candlestick chart, which covers a much shorter time span as a consequence but gives a clear overall picture.

Renko Charts

Another charting variant that has some similarities to the three-line break chart is called the Renko chart. The Renko chart has a procedure to only plot new lines when the prices demand it, as with the three-line break chart, so again, the horizontal axis does not reflect any consistent time scale. There is much more regularity to the chart, however, as it uses standard lengths of lines.

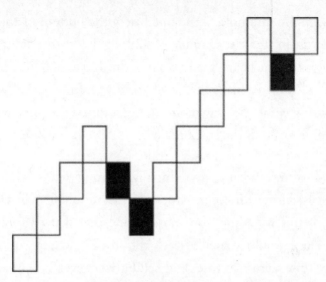

Example of a Renko Chart

As stated, the charting rules are similar to the three-line break, with the exception that you require the values to achieve certain thresholds before you plot them — it is not sufficient for the value to simply exceed the last high in order to plot a white line; it must reach the next number in the series, so that a whole line can be drawn.

The values are again based on the closing prices, as there is no provision to show additional prices. The threshold values correspond to a regular spacing. For instance, the values may be every $5, and say the current price was $16 in an uptrend. The last line drawn would have been a white line from $10 to $15. When the closing price reaches $20, and not before, another line can be added to the chart. A value of $19.50 would not be sufficient, and the chart would not change. If the price jumped up to $28 in one leap, then two lines would be drawn for that day — one from $15 to $20, and one from $20 to $25, which would be the highest threshold value exceeded. The lines would be drawn corner to corner, and not stacked, even though they were for the same day.

For a reversal, the threshold is the one below the bottom of the last line. In other words, for the last example of $28, the lower threshold would be $15, as that is the one below the bottom of the $20 to $25 line. If the price went below $15, then a black line would be drawn from $20 down to $15. In fact, nothing would be drawn on this chart unless the price went below $15 — or above $30, if the stock rallied.

The purpose of the chart is again to highlight strong trends, while ignoring brief reversals. Using different values for the threshold will change the sensitivity of this function. You can imagine that if the threshold were small, the chart would virtually track the stock price, so you would be buying any time the price rose, and selling whenever the price dropped — very basic trend following, likely to result in much trading and not much profit. On the other hand, if the threshold value is too large, then you have the issue of only discovering the trend and trading after the first major price gains have occurred. What you have is a smoothing function that relies on a trend, and one that lasts for a while, to give any chance of trading profit.

In use, you would experiment with the size of the threshold value so that you did not jump on too many minor trends that reversed, but found a sufficient number of trading opportunities that worked out. Using other indicators in conjunction with the Renko chart would be advisable.

Again, Renko charts are available for those who would like to explore this systematic, orderly charting technique. The Renko chart for an Apple® computer, equivalent to the chart given before, follows.

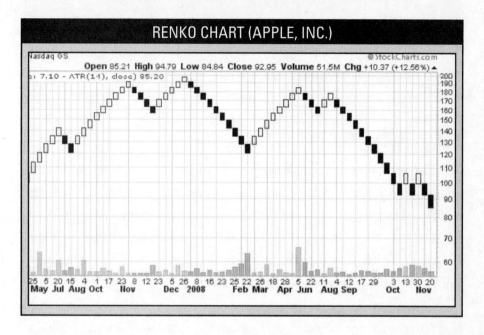

Notice that the timescales do not match, because of the system and laws by which the chart is drawn. You can see that it gives a clear indication of major trend directions, simplifying the moves of the stock price over two years into one chart. It is interesting to look at the time scale, as the chart at first glance appears to be equally divided between uptrend and downtrend.

This is a function of the way the chart is generated, as the equal steps of Renko charting require it. However, look at the rally starting around November 23 near the middle of the chart. This lasted for about a month, with a downtrend commencing in December. Two months saw this downtrend reverse again, but the following rally, which actually appears smaller, took twice as long. The appearance is driven by the price points and nothing else. The recent price crash in September 2008 was dominating, but only one month long.

While this seems strange to the eye, which is used to conventional charting methods, it is actually the strength of the Renko chart, as trends are spotted regardless of time, with a greater clarity. With a suitably large threshold value, the chart does not give any negative signals during a large trend, and thus, does not cause confusion.

Kagi Charts

Another interesting variation on price charting is the kagi chart, which also originates in Japan and is believed to have been used when the Japanese stock market started trading in the 1870s. Steve Nison introduced them to the Western trader in *Beyond Candlesticks: New Japanese Charting Techniques Revealed* in 1994. Similar to the previous variations of the Three-Line Break and Renko charts, in that the time scale is not regularly spaced but arises from the price action, the kagi uses lines of two different thicknesses instead of rectangles to represent the movement of the values. It is also possible to generate kagi charts with two different line colors, rather than thicknesses, and **www.StockCharts.com** has this facility, but for publishing clarity, this book will only show the varying thicknesses.

First, kagi charts only use the closing prices. Unlike candlesticks, they have no graphic facility to include other information and are a "big picture" price and timing tool, rather than one that gives the day-to-day psychological nuances of the candlestick chart.

Second, and in common with the previous alternate charting methods, kagi charts deal with price "lumps," that is, the price has to move a certain amount before there is any need to draw another line. This concept contributes to the outcome shared with those methods where the timescale has no standard period.

Kagi charting is another method of drawing the price fluctuations that identify the trend in the stock price, and thus, it indicates which way to go and when you should be in the market. The basic idea that this is built on is that a trend will continue until there is a reason for it to stop or reverse. Kagi charting provides a visual identification of the direction and continuity of the trend.

The procedure for kagi charting starts with determining the minimum size of price movement that you will need in order to draw a reversal. This can be an absolute amount, which you would select relative to the actual share price, or it can be a percentage, so that it adjusts as the price varies to always maintain the same relationship. A typical percentage may be 3 or 4 percent, and if you choose a value instead, it should be in line with this.

The reason that you have a minimum size is to avoid having frequent changes in trend direction, but if the size is too large, then you will get fewer indications and may miss some price movement. The choice should be made while considering the actual security you are tracking, as some fluctuate more than others.

A thick line is generally associated with an uptrending market, and a thinner line signifies a downward tendency. The rules for drawing the lines are as follows.

Vertical lines represent price action, and horizontal lines called "inflection lines" connect movement in different directions. Suppose the closing price goes up from a starting or base price, then it will be represented as a thick vertical line which stops at the incremental amount. Referring to Figure 9, if the base price is $15, and the closing price on the next day is $16.50, with a reversal increment of $1, you would draw a thick vertical line from $15 (point A) to $16 (point B) — the nearest increment. As long as the closing price on the following days varied between $15.01 and $16.99, there would be nothing further added to the chart.

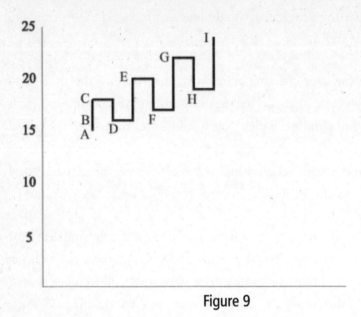

Figure 9

Suppose that the price then rose to $18.25; the thick line would be continued up to $18 (point C) as shown. Now the price has to exceed $19 or be less than $17 for anything further to be drawn.

Prices in an uptrend commonly progress by making higher highs and higher lows, so assume that over the next few days or weeks, when the price movements are sufficient to warrant further drawing, the following values are plotted — $16 (D), $20 (E), $17 (F), $22 (G), $19 (H), and $24 (I) — and these are shown on the figure.

So far, this has shown a simple uptrend, with higher highs and higher lows, and has all been drawn with the thicker line. The chart continues with the prices plotted as shown, and the rule for line thickness, which gives an indication of the trend, is that the thickness changes to a thin line when the line must extend below the last low, and changes back to a thick line when the line subsequently extends above the last high.

The last low was at $19 (H). If the next value to be plotted is $16, then the line down is drawn thick to $19, and extended as a thin line to $16 (J), as seen in Figure 10.

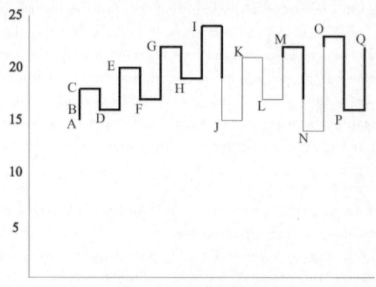

Figure 10

As shown, the line continues to be drawn thin while fluctuating up and down, at values of $21 (K) and $17 (L). As the next point, M at $22, is above the last high at K, the line changes back to being thick when it exceeds $21. Straight away, the next low at N is lower than the last low at L, so the line changes back to thin when it passes the level of L, $17 — and so the pattern goes.

The system of drawing a kagi chart is mechanical, and the only decision is how large an increment to use. When the line is thick or bold, then the chart is indicating an uptrend, and when the line is thin, it suggests a downtrend is in effect. If the price is not trending, then the line thickness will vary often, and this charting method is not suitable for trading when there is no trend. However, with defined trends, the kagi chart, in its simplest application, gives buy and sell signals at the point where the line thickness changes. Where the line changes from thin to thick, then an upward trend is indicated, and you may buy the stock. If the line changes back to thin, then you sell.

When the line is consistently thick, then it indicates that a strong rally is in place, making higher highs and higher lows. If the line is thin, then that indicates a decline, with lower lows and lower highs. Alternating thick and thin lines show that the market is in equilibrium, and there is no definite trend in place. As such, the kagi chart gives a method of seeing whether there is a trend in the market, which filters out the noise of day-to-day fluctuations and provides an alternative to the commonly used simple moving average.

The kagi chart is relatively unknown to many traders, and, as it does provide a way to ignore unimportant moves in the market and focus on the true trend, it can be a useful tool. It is a true price chart, and hence, can have the various charting techniques applied. For instance, you can draw a trendline on a kagi chart by connecting successive lows, as previously described. Some analysts will also look at the number of higher highs that a kagi chart has seen and be wary that there may be a market correction due after eight or ten highs.

The kagi chart can be used along with the candlestick methods, as the two techniques complement each other. Kagi charting is good at showing the underlying market movement and can be refined easily to suit the security being traded to virtually eliminate false swings by changing the increment. The candlestick chart shows the daily market sentiment so that the moment to trade and follow the trend can be defined.

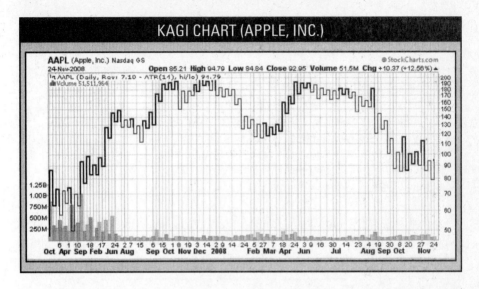

The kagi chart covers a similar period to the previous Renko chart, but if you compare them, you will notice that they present the price information in a radically different way. For the increment chosen, the kagi chart shows some areas that would not be profitable to trade, as they turn out as sideways movement. This serves to show the importance of experimenting with each technique and trying different values to see whether it can suit your needs.

Candle Volume Charts

Candle volume charts present an interesting alternative to the conventional charts discussed in the main section. In the same way that the candlestick chart can improve understanding over the simple bar chart, the candle volume chart assists consideration of the elements of a candlestick chart with an attached trading volume chart.

Stuart McPhee is a successful trader and coach, and his book offers excellent advice on developing your plan and your mindset. In the following case study, he emphasizes the importance of looking at the trading volumes in your assessment of the commitment of the market to the signals that you are observing.

CASE STUDY: STUART MCPHEE

Stuart McPhee is a private trader, author, and trading coach. He has written numerous articles and texts, most recently *Trading in a Nutshell, 3rd Edition*. He also conducts trading courses throughout southeast Asia and has presented at trading expos throughout Australia and in Singapore, Kuala Lumpur, Ho Chi Minh City, Mumbai, Dalian, Shenzhen, and Bangkok.

Visit Stuart's "Develop your Trading Plan" Web site (**www.trading-plan. com**) for detailed information on how to develop a trading plan that is right for you and that you will implement with confidence.

What type of trading do you use candlesticks with — what markets and time periods?

When you have a style of trading where timing is critical, it is important to have an effective method of monitoring price action. For example, with my conservative, medium-term approach, which I trade through my superannuation (retirement) fund, I trade equities on the Australian Securities Exchange (ASX) from mainly the top 500 companies.

As I am trading medium-term trends, the timing of my entry is not overly critical — as long as I enter within the prevailing medium-term uptrend.

However, I also trade Contracts for Difference (CFDs) on a limited number of top 50 stocks on the ASX. For this style of trading, timing is much more critical, as you want to take as much advantage as you can of the short-term trend, which may only last a few days.

I have found certain short-term reversal signals to be quite effective, as these form the basis of my entry conditions for my short-term trading.

CASE STUDY: STUART MCPHEE

When and how did you start getting interested in trading?

It was back in 1996 when my wife and I had some savings and wanted to do something with it. We didn't consider property at that stage and almost automatically considered the stock market. We went to a broker to set up an account and, in the early stages, considered their advice to be golden. It would have been soon after that I thought how I could probably do the analysis myself and have more of an influence over what we were buying and selling.

Did you use candlestick charts from the start of your trading? If not, how much difference do you think they made to your trades when you learned to interpret them?

Yes, when I was first introduced to charting, the first charts I was shown were with candlesticks. Furthermore, all of the short-term patterns I was shown were candlesticks, and they were all given their various names.

I believe the reason I was shown them was the clear way in which they represented the data from a day's trading. I remember thinking how clearly they painted the picture of what had happened during the trading period and how effective they may be.

Furthermore, when you consider how sensory we are as humans, and how much better we understand things when we see them, it is easy to see why so many people prefer candlesticks, due to the clear picture of trading action they show.

Do you enter a trade on the basis of a candlestick pattern only — always, sometimes, or never?

For my short-term trading, even though the actual reversal pattern is the key condition for my entry, it must be accompanied by other conditions, like volume and ensuring that the medium-term trend is also heading in the same direction as the short-term trend I am about to enter.

So whilst it is key, I wouldn't enter a trade purely on the candlestick pattern and ignore other conditions.

CASE STUDY: STUART MCPHEE

What other indicators do you use in conjunction with candlesticks if you want confirmation? Which do you find work best in combination with candle signals?

Only one. Earlier on, I went through the search, looking for the right indicator to use, and every time I heard someone else present a seminar about trading, I ended up considering the indicators that the presenter had on his charts during the presentation. I used to think like many people do, and that is, "if he is using them, then they must work, so I am going to use them."

There are many popular indicators that are widely used, like the MACD, stochastic oscillator, relative strength index, directional movement, and the list goes on. However, I don't use any of them and haven't for a number of years now.

I am not saying that the indicators above don't work, or they won't assist you with your trading. I have challenged the various indicators to see whether they would provide me a significant advantage in my trading, and for me, they all came up with a negative response. I therefore questioned the need to use any of them in my trading. The truth is that no indicator is infallible, and they will often provide a false signal. If they don't provide a marked advantage to you, if they don't provide you an edge, then why use them?

The only indicators I use are a moving average and a couple of simple indicators I developed myself, and their use is limited to my entry decision. The whole premise behind my use of indicators is to keep it simple.

So with regard to my short-term trading, whilst I need the relevant reversal pattern to exist, one of the other conditions I need is for the medium-term trend to also be heading in the same direction as the short-term trend I am about to enter. To do this, I will use a moving average.

CASE STUDY: STUART MCPHEE

Do you use and find filters, such as price or volume, effective in assisting selection of worthwhile candlestick patterns?

Volume is often a misunderstood and/or underestimated piece of trading data. It can provide useful insight into the behavior of market participants, demonstrating the commitment of buyers and sellers and providing further evidence of other analysis you are conducting.

For example, when seeking to confirm a particular candlestick pattern you have identified, an indication of relatively strong volume would add further evidence and strengthen your reasons for buying.

I use the term "relatively strong volume" because the volume during the period the pattern has occurred can be compared with their average daily or weekly volume in the recent past. Where you see a significant increase in volume supporting a move in the price, that could add weight to the pattern you have identified.

There are many named candlestick patterns. Do you find that you only focus on a few, and if so, which?

I generally only focus on a few, and they are all short-term reversal patterns — patterns like hammers, bullish and bearish engulfing patterns, and bullish and bearish haramis and doji. They all show a potential reversal which can often be confirmed the next day.

In my time trading short-term trends, I have found these to be very effective at identifying the changes in short-term trends, and I have developed a great deal of trust in them. They are not perfect, of course, but quite useful.

Knowledge of the trading volume always gives improvement to your stock selection, and there is reference to high and low trading volumes in some of the candlestick patterns given. Frequently, we concentrate on the price movement and overlook the messages that we can derive from knowing the volume of trading. The candle volume chart puts the volume information as part of the price information so that it is impossible to overlook.

There is a saying that volume precedes price. While there are some who would disagree with that, it appears that at least the higher volumes occur at times when the prices are active and low volumes are associated with a deteriorating trend. Volume spikes show a high level of trading interest in the stock.

The volume information is incorporated into the candlestick chart by making the width of the candles proportional to the trading volume on the day. This means that candle volume charts again do not keep a regular scale for the horizontal date axis, as a wide candle representing large trading volume will push the rest of the candles farther over. This does enforce the emphasis that the candlestick should have.

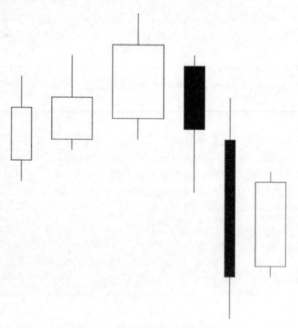

Example of Candle Volume Chart

This sample chart shows an increasing price and volume, culminating in a fat white candle at the peak. The following two bearish candles have reducing volumes, which reflect a lack of trading interest.

There are some guidelines to reading candle volume charts. As mentioned, when volume is increasing, price is also usually increasing in a bullish market, and the opposite is true — a bearish market often has both volume and price reducing. If a bullish move is not supported by an increasing or large volume, you should beware if you are long, and look for a bearish signal for going short.

The reason for this is that the market is showing no enthusiasm. The rise in prices is from a lack of sellers, rather than any great eagerness by buyers, and when the prices get high enough, more sellers may suddenly hit the market, and the prices decline with increased volume.

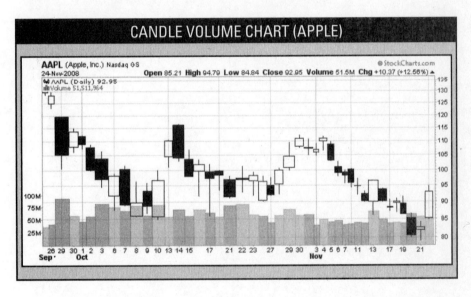

Because of the thickness of the candles, the candle volume chart shown covers a much smaller time than the previous systems, although it does compare with the original candlestick chart of Apple®. In view of the significance of volume in interpreting the validity of the candlestick signals, as attested to by several correspondents, this chart is a substitute for the regular candlestick chart that, with reading practice, would save more time in confirming the trends.

● SAFETY ZONE ●

If you have never done it before, when you venture into the world of trading, you will discover new things about yourself. Some you may not like, such as the first time you do not sell when you know you should, and lose more than you needed to — and we have all done that at some time. It is not lack of knowledge that causes many traders to take a while to become profitable, but an inability to cope with the mental battle. By working on your emotions and your money management, you will shortcut the learning curve. Good luck, and good trading.

Appendix A:
Practice Charts

To help you understand how to read charts and candlestick patterns, included are some annotated company charts in this appendix.

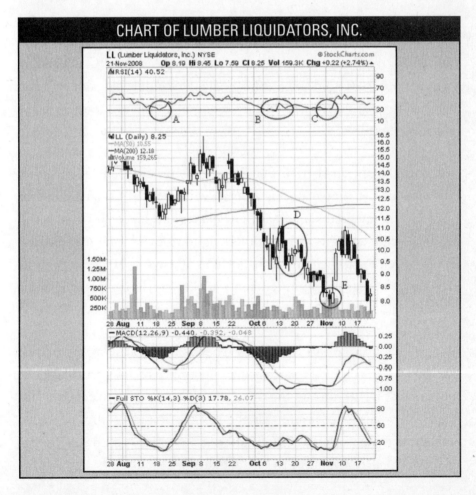

CHART OF LUMBER LIQUIDATORS, INC.

Chart of Lumber Liquidators Inc.

First, take time to note all the oscillators that are included. I am not suggesting that you need to have all these present at one time, as I believe that would be more likely to confuse than help, but they are included to allow you to form a sense of how they work together and indicate the condition of the market. In your trading, you will decide on one or two that are most meaningful to the time and security that you are looking at and learn those thoroughly. Charts in this customizable form are available from **www.StockCharts.com**, and you may also subscribe to have access to additional features.

The relative strength index, or indicator, is plotted across the top of the chart. The overbought and oversold lines are set at values of 30 and 70, and you can see that the 30 line is touched at points A, B, and C, suggesting that the stock is oversold and due for a rally. This it duly did, although you will see that the two rallies at B, corresponding to the two touches to the line, were short lived.

The center chart, apart from showing the candlesticks, includes further information. Two simple moving averages with periods of 50 and 200 days are plotted as lines across the chart. The darker line, based 200 days, is still in an uptrend, and this indicates the long-term trend. The intermediate trend is given by the lighter line, which uses 50 days — 10 weeks — as its basis, and it is clearly in decline, as most stocks were during this time of the market crash of 2008.

Along the bottom of this chart are a series of bars that show the trading volumes. These can be a check on the significance of any particular price move noted. Depending on the size of the account, some traders will also screen on volumes to ensure that the stock is liquid — that is, traded enough that you can always enter and exit a position, and prices are not unduly influenced by one or two large trades.

Below the main chart, you will see first the MACD. This is a trend-following indicator and not as jumpy as the RSI. If you look carefully, you will see that it appears to react a little more slowly than the RSI. The balanced position for this indicator is at the zero level. When the line is above this, the price is usually in an uptrend, and you will be looking for a long position. As the line is below zero for the greater part of this time period, it indicates a decline, which is what you will see if you look at the candlestick chart.

There are two lines on the MACD, and the main line is the darker one. The lighter one is the signal line, which is actually the nine-day exponential moving average (EMA) of the main line. If trading with the MACD, some traders will buy when the line rises above the zero line, out of the oversold territory, and sell short when the line crosses below; other traders use the signal line crossing the main line, so that when the signal crosses down below the main line, they buy long, and when the signal line rises above the main line, they sell short.

Below this, at the bottom of the figure, you can see the stochastic indicator. This, again, is generally faster than the MACD. In this particular case, that looks like an advantage, but you should realize that in some markets and securities, a slower indicator might work better by not giving a signal too early and having you trade on a false move, which you would be stopped out of.

The stochastic has preset levels of 20 and 80, which are generally accepted oversold and overbought values. The main line is the %K, and the signal line is called %D, which is actually a moving average of %K, in the example based on three days, which is a fairly standard figure.

In use, you might buy when the %K drops below 20 percent, then hooks back up, which indicates that the stock is oversold but may be coming back. Sell, or go short, when the opposite happens — that is, the value goes above 80 percent and hooks back down. This is a common use for the oscillator.

The signal line can also give the trigger for a trade, in a similar way to that on the MACD. When the signal line drops below the main %K line, then you can enter a long trade. When the signal goes above the main line, you exit the trade, if that is the way your trading plan is assembled, or you may use this as a signal to go short.

With the clearer uptrends on the figure, you can see that each of these oscillators could on its own have given you a signal that would provide a profitable trade. However, you are well advised to get at least two indications before trading, as this confirms the chances of success.

Not all signals are good for trading when taken on their own. The August stochastic would have scored well by indicating a long trade on the hook up (20th), signal crossing (21st), or the rising through the 20 percent line (22nd), whichever your trading plan used as an entry signal. If you used just one of these indications in October, your trade might not have been so good. There was a hook up on the 3rd and the 9th, and in each case, the next day was down. The signal line crossed on the 6th, and the next day was down. On the 10th, the %K line rose above 20 percent, and this would have been in profit on the next day, although subsequent events might have made this also a losing trade.

If you were following the candlesticks, how would you have fared? The short body on the 7th was an Inverted Hammer, but the open on the 8th was much lower, so you would have suspected that the reversal was not ready. Despite the low open, the stock gained significantly to finish the day as a bullish engulfing signal, which would have you watching the next day for confirmation that a rally was coming.

This time on the next day, the stock opened lower, and closed down, denying the rally, and you can see that the last three days had long upper shadows, which suggests that the bulls had been trying to lift the price, but that it had not stuck. In general, the candlesticks give an indication that there is no overriding force, and that the signals from the oscillators may not give the expected results.

Because you understand the psychology of the candlesticks, you would be able to assess this day by day and avoid plunging in too quickly. That is not to say that you cannot be fooled by the candle patterns too when they do not continue as expected, but they give you a different and better perspective on the market sentiment.

The patterns of D work more as expected, with a Bullish Harami that is not confirmed. The Spinning Top on the 20th is significant because a small body has a high volume, and the Bearish Engulfing signal that comes on the next day is proved to be valid. Although this is not confirmed by the values of the oscillators, you can see that a hook back down on the stochastic is a bearish sign.

If you missed trading on this, at least you would not miss at E the Bullish Engulfing on November 3 and 4, accompanied by high volume, which shows that the pattern is significant. With the extremely oversold position indicated by the oscillators, it is no surprise that the rally is strong, if short-lived.

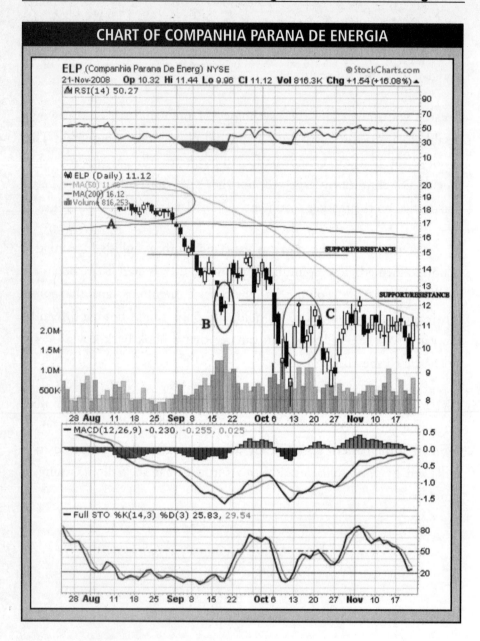

CHART OF COMPANHIA PARANA DE ENERGIA

Chart of Companhia Parana De Energia

A second practice chart will serve to emphasize the importance of volume in determining which are important candle signals. Looking first at area A, you can see many candlesticks that you may think are significant because they have short or doji bodies. As you can see from the price action, there are some minor price movements, but for the most part, the price is staying around the same level and trading in that range.

If you now look at the bottom of the chart, you can see that the stochastic shows the stock oversold, which would normally indicate that a rally is due. Plainly, this did not occur. This chart shows how a little knowledge may be a dangerous thing. Without looking at the overall picture, you might be tempted to trade based on the candlesticks indicating a bullish reversal, on the basis of the stochastic passing up through the 20 percent level, or on the signal line crossing on August 20.

While there might have been some profit to be taken within the trading range, the price did not move greatly. If you examine the chart, you will find that the volume of trading was light during this period, and this suggests that the signals given are not as strong as they would otherwise be.

Contrast this with September 18, area B, the highest volume on this chart. This day is a Hammer, so even though this is a high-volume day, it is also a short real body day. A high volume with little difference between the opening and closing prices is meaningful, and the following price action demonstrates this with a rapid rally.

Area C also has reasonable volumes and clear signals. The Hanging Man is followed a few days later by a Bullish Harami as the price fluctuates on this section of the chart.

This chart has also been annotated with a couple of support and resistance lines. These can be used to help determine price targets. The detailed discussion of these is beyond the scope of this book, but it is found that quite often, what was a support becomes a resistance line and what was a resistance line becomes as support, as the price moves from one section of the chart to another.

The first line, at $14.80, was a minor support in the decline through the beginning of September. This was tested as a resistance on the 12th, with the upper shadow reaching for it before the decline continued. Note the Tweezer Top at the same level on September 25 and 26, where the resistance level held strong.

The lower support/resistance level is at $12.20. Shadows touched it on September 18, 19, and 29, and then it was tested by the market to be a resistance on October 14, a large volume day. In view of that, it was a reasonable target for the rally at the end of October, which it hit with just a minor break. While it is certainly easier to tell where the support and resistance are after they have been tested several times, if you familiarize yourself with any particular chart, you should learn to see them after just a couple of indications.

With Internet access, there is nothing to stop you from printing out several charts, such as those above, and looking at them in detail to become familiar with the actions of the market. While there are many times when you can see how the candlestick patterns are predictive, you should also note where they did not work and try to work out why they may have failed. Do not obsess about this, as the markets will not totally yield to analysis, and you will always be able to find exceptions; but note whether there are known issues, such as low volume or other contraindications, as this will enable you to be better at spotting and understanding them when you are trading.

Once you have familiarized yourself with this exercise, you may also want to print out some charts at random and lay a blank sheet of paper over them. Then, withdraw the paper, day-by-day, to the right, and each day, try to guess where the price will go on the next day. By doing such exercises, you will become a better trader.

Appendix B: Resources

There are many books and Web sites offering information on candlestick charting and trading in general. There are also many exaggerated claims for trading systems and information, which should be viewed with caution. There is no Holy Grail for trading, and the more you make yourself informed about how to trade, the better your hope for success.

I do not know of any successful trader who does not have an extensive library, and a thirst for knowledge will assist you in becoming better qualified. As stated in the beginning, the short-term trader relies largely on being on the right side of a trade when someone else is on the wrong side. Therefore, it only makes good sense to keep your education up to date, and absorb as much information as you can, to stay ahead of other traders. The resources listed here are ones that I have personally used and can recommend.

Books

The Candlestick Course

Steve Nison

Nison is rightly considered the granddaddy of candlestick charting, having discovered and brought it to the Western world. He continues to provide information and support, and studying any book by him will be rewarding. He also offers courses on DVD.

Candlestick Charting Explained

Gregory L. Morris

Morris has been involved with candlesticks nearly as long as Nison, visiting Japan in 1992 to find out more. This book, which runs more than 500 pages long, is a good resource.

Candlesticks Explained

Martin J. Pring

This book contains many example charts, along with a wealth of information and includes a multimedia CD-ROM that provides a presentation of the material to reinforce learning.

In the field of more general trading information, I recommend:

The Complete Guide to Investing in Short-Term Trading

Alan Northcott

A natural recommendation, as this was my first book about trading.

Short-Term Trading in the New Stock Market

Toni Turner

I find all of Turner's books very readable and packed with information. This book has 14 pages of candle matters and covers many other strategies, in addition to the psychology of trading.

Trading in a Nutshell

Stuart McPhee

McPhee's book, now in its third edition, is advice from a practical trader, covering not only psychology but touching on physical fitness, too, which is easily overlooked in the trading world. It also includes plenty of sound trading advice. Based in Australia, McPhee is invited to speak around the world.

How I Made $2,000,000 in the Stock Market

Nicholas Darvas

Written in 1960, this book is one of the classics of trading, telling how an itinerant dancer made a great deal of money on the stock market by applying what amounts to common sense. His story is a great example of how simplicity can be key to a winning system.

Web sites

There seem to be more Web sites springing up every day, and a Google™ search for candlestick charting reveals 608,000 hits. A short list of Web sites dedicated to candlesticks would include the following.

www.candlecharts.com

Nison's Web site, and therefore, an authority for all candlestick matters.

www.hotcandlestick.com

A Web site devoted to candlesticks.

www.profitablecandlestickcharting.com

A comprehensive, educational resource.

Appendix C: Glossary

ADX: stands for average directional movement index; an indicator that shows the strength of the movement of a price

AMEX: the American Stock Exchange, which trades stocks that are too small for the NYSE

Ask Price: the price at which you can buy a stock on the market; what the brokers are asking for it

Back-test: using historical data to test the performance of a trading plan

Bar Charts: price graphs that show the information as a vertical bar

Bear Market: a market where prices are falling

Bearish Candle: a candle where the price falls between the open and the close of the period, usually black or red

Bearish Reversal Pattern: a candlestick formation in an uptrending market that implies that the trend will cease and the price go down

Bears: traders and investors who believe that the price of a stock is too high, and reduce the value

Bid Price: the price at which a stock can be sold in the market

Blended Candle: reducing several candlesticks down to one summary candle

Box Theory: popularized by Nicholas Darvas, a way of looking at stock price movements

Breakout: when a price has been in a limited range, a breakout occurs when it moves outside that range

Broker: a dealer in stocks and other securities

Bull Market: a market where prices are rising

Bullish Candle: a candle where the price rises during the day, or time period; it is often represented as white or green

Bullish Reversal Pattern: a candlestick formation that occurs in a bear market and is considered to be signaling a reverse in the downtrend and the start of rising prices

Bulls: traders and investors who believe that the stock should increase in price

Candle Patterns: several consecutive candles in a certain formation

Call: a type of option that gives the right to buy a stock at a set price up until a certain date

Candlestick: or candle, is the basic shape of the indicator on the price graph. Typically, it looks like a candle with a wick at one or both ends

CFD: stands for contract for difference, a financial instrument that is similar to an option

Closing Price: the last price for the security, equity, or other financial instrument when the market closes the session

Commodities: a physical substance that is traded, or bought and sold on a market. Includes grains, livestock, energy, and metals

Continuation Signal: indication that a current trend, which may be either up or down, will continue

Day Trader: a trader who is trading for the shortest possible time spans, from seconds to minutes or hours, but never holding a trade overnight

Derivative: a financial instrument that derives its value from something else, such as an option or future

Diverge: go in opposite direction from

Doji: a candlestick where the opening price and closing price are the same, so the real body has no length

Downday: a day of trading where the price finishes lower than it started

Downtrend: a long period of time over which the price is falling on average

Engulf: of candlesticks, refers to the candlestick real body being longer than the one previous, with a higher high and a lower low

Equities: another word for stocks

ETF: stands for exchange traded fund, which is a basket of shares or securities in a particular market

Exit Point: is the value at which you have decided that you will sell your stock and exit the trade

Exponential Moving Average: a value calculated from a stated number of previous periods, which is calculated so that the later periods have a greater effect on the value

Fibonacci: an Italian mathematician, also known as Leonardo of Pisa; a mathematical series where each successive term is the sum of the two previous terms

Fill: the term for your order to buy or sell shares to be completed; e.g., your order is filled

Forex: derives for Foreign Exchange, and identifies the marketplace for buying and selling the currencies of different countries

Fundamental Analysis: refers to valuing a company from its financial information, using revenues, capitalization, expenditures, and other means

Futures: a contract to buy or sell a commodity or security for a predetermined price at a set time in the future

Gap: there is a gap between two successive candles if the real bodies do not overlap; sometimes can also include a gap between shadows

High: is the top of the bar or candlestick, and so the top of the upper shadow, if there is one

High Wave Candle: has a short body and long shadows

Indicator: in trading, an indicator is derived from previous market pricing, and is an attempt to point toward the expected future price movement

Intraday: price movement during the day, essential to a day trader

Investor: a person or institution that buys a security with the intention of keeping it for a length of time in expectation of the price increasing

Level II: defines a certain amount of detail of the market trading, showing individual trading action rather than just a bid price and an ask price

Leverage: multiplies the amount you have invested, as when trading the ForEx or options, so that a small increase in price gives a larger return

Limit order: an order to your broker that limits the price at which you are prepared to buy or sell a stock

Line Chart: a basic price chart, with a line drawn through the closing price on each day or time period

Liquidity: a measure of the amount of trading in a stock; good liquidity means it is easy to buy and sell

Long: to be long in a stock means to buy it

Long Black Line: refers to a long bearish candlestick, at least two or three times as long as the typical length for the security

Long White Line: a bullish candlestick that is two or three times longer than the typical length on the chart

Low: the cheapest price of the day for the stock or security; the bottom of the lower shadow

Lower Shadow: on a candlestick, the line projecting down from the real body

MACD: stands for Moving Average Convergence/Divergence, an indicator created from moving average figures

Margin: a facility given to traders to borrow money from the broker

Market order: an order to your broker to buy or sell shares at the best price he can in the market at that time

Marubozu: a special candlestick that has no upper or lower shadow, it is just the real body

Momentum: one of the factors that may be considered when selecting your trades; indicators provide a measure of the speed of price change

Moving Average: an average of a declared number of periods that is updated when each new period occurs

NASDAQ: an electronic stock market, mainly known for trading technology stocks

NYSE: the New York Stock Exchange, one of the most significant stock exchanges in the world

OHLC: stands for open/high/low/close, the four fundamental prices used to define a bar or a candlestick. The term OHLC is often used as shorthand for the type of bar chart that shows these figures

Open: the first traded price of the day or other time period

Option: an option allows a buyer the option to buy a share at a predetermined price within a set period, or to sell a share at a predetermined price within the time — there is no obligation to do so if it would not benefit the purchaser of the option

Option Holder: the buyer of the option

Option Writer: the seller of an option, receives payment in return for the obligation of fulfilling the option if required

Order: an instruction to your broker to deal in shares on your behalf

Oscillator: a general term for an indicator that oscillates, or goes up and down within a range of values, usually indicating the amount of enthusiasm for the stock and its price

Overbought: a stock is considered overbought if it has been subject to keen buying, which has increased its price, possibly to a level that is not sustainable

Oversold: when oversold, a stock has been losing value as shareholders have decided to sell, and it may reach a point where the price has dropped lower than the real value, suggesting that there may be a rise in price to come

Pivot Point: a pivot point is where a trend changes from bullish to bearish or vice versa, and occurs at the shift in sentiment toward the security

Premium: the amount paid for an option

Put: a type of option; the right to sell a stock at a predetermined price by a set date

Real Body: of a candlestick is the rectangle that forms the middle, between the opening price and the closing price; it is usually white or black

Resistance Line: can be drawn on a price chart and represents a line above which the fluctuating price will not go, for the current perception of the stock

Reversal Signal: an indication that the current trend, whether for the price to increase or reduce, may reverse and become the opposite

Risk/Reward: every trade should be evaluated for its financial risk and reward, the risk being the most you think you can lose if you have made a bad selection, and the reward being the expected profit, if your choice is good

RSI: stands for relative strength indicator; it is a momentum indicator that compares the strength of upward moves with downward moves, and charts the result

Selling Short: a method of profiting from the loss in price of a stock, essentially from initially selling shares you do not own, then replacing them later by buying them at the then current price, which you hope is lower

Shadow: on a candlestick, it is the line sticking up and down from the real body

Shares: constitute ownership in a company, which issues thousands of shares and receives money for them in the initial public offering, after which, the shares are traded between individuals

Shaven Bottom: a candlestick that has no lower shadow

Shaven Head: a candlestick that has no upper shadow

Short: to be short is the opposite of being long, and means that you owe someone shares, and are hoping to profit from the price going down before you deliver them

Short-Term Trader: buys and sells stocks and shares or other financial securities with the intention of making a profit within days or weeks

Signal Line: a line on an indicator that can provide a signal for when to trade, commonly by crossing another line

Simple Moving Average: is calculated from day to day for a specified number of previous time periods, and is the sum of the values divided by the number of periods

Spinning Top: one of the standard candlestick forms, it has a short real body and can be thought of as looking like a child's top

Spread: the difference between the bid and ask prices

Star: a generic candlestick pattern form which comprises long real bodies and spinning tops, the top gapping away from the long body appearing like a star in the sky

Stochastic Oscillator: an indicator that compares a stock's closing price to the range of price in a set number of periods

Stocks: another word for shares; generally used interchangeably, although stocks can describe shares in several different companies

Stock Market: may be a physical place, but is increasingly an electronic system where stocks can be bought and sold

Stop-Loss: a term for an order to sell shares to avoid losses that are too great, if the price does not go in the desired direction

Stopping Out: when you reach a price at which your stocks are sold

Strike price: the pre-agreed share price in an option trade

Support And Resistance: imaginary boundaries on the price chart between which the price is expected to fluctuate for the time being; see support line and resistance line

Support Line: can be drawn on a price chart below the current prices, and represents the value that the price is not expected to go below, based on price history

Swing Trading: similar to short-term trading in that the goal is to profit in a relatively short period of time, typically holding stocks for two to five days

Technical Analysis: is concerned with short-term movements in price caused by trading sentiments, which may be discerned by using indicators and candlestick patterns; does not look at the long term value of a company, as does fundamental analysis

Trading Plan: is important, especially for novices, to avoid emotional decisions that may not be beneficial

Trailing Stop: a type of order that sets a moving value for a rising stock to be sold at if the price falls; the value is adjusted with the rising price to safeguard the gains

Trend: showing a general and consistent movement in price, either up or down

Trending: a stock is trending if it is showing a trend, which is the price moving in a definite direction, not just up and down

Trendline: a straight line that can be subjectively drawn on a price chart to show the general direction

Trigger: a sign that a trade should be placed, and can be derived from indicators and/or pattern observation

Upday: a day when the closing price is higher than the opening price

Upper Shadow: the line up from the real body of a candlestick, the top of the upper shadow is the highest price reached during the day

Uptrend: is in place when a stock's price is consistently moving upwards

Volatility: a measure of the fluctuations in the price of a financial instrument

Volume: the number of shares traded in the period, which provides an indication of the strength of traders' feelings

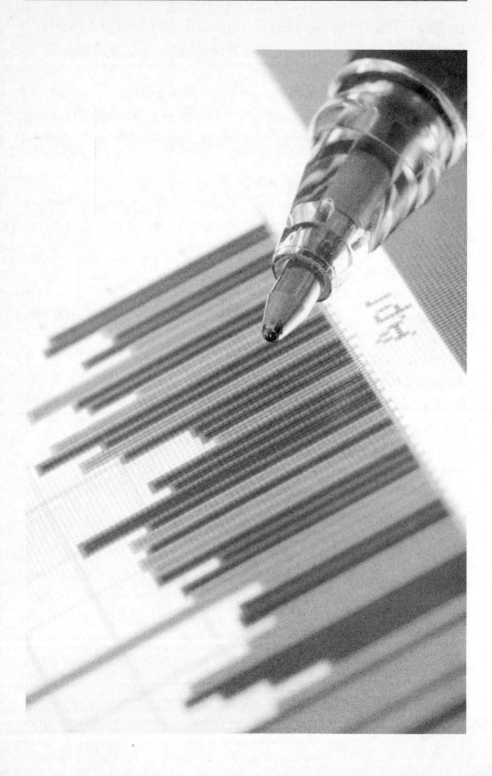

# Author Dedication & Biography

Dedicated to my beautiful wife Liz, my constant companion through life's adventures and strength for more than 30 years.

Alan Northcott is a successful financial author, freelance writer, trader, professional engineer, and farmer, along with other pursuits, and he now lives in the Midwest. Originating from England, he immigrated with his wife to America in 1992. His engineering career spanned more than 30 years on both sides of the Atlantic, and recent years have found him seeking and living a more diverse, fulfilling life style.

This is his third financial book, and his previous works, *Asset Protection for Business Owners and High Income Earners: How to Protect What You Own from Lawsuits and Creditors* and *The Complete Guide to Investing in Short Term Trading: How to Earn High Rates of Returns Safely* are also available from Atlantic Publishing Company (**www.atlantic-pub.com**). He offers a free newsletter on various related topics. You can find out more at **www. alannorthcott.com**, or e-mail him directly at alannorthcott@msn.com.

Index

A

ADX, 273
AMEX, 273
Ask Price, 273, 276

B

Backtest, 273
Bear Market, 273-274, 214, 234, 45, 77, 85, 106
Bearish Candle, 273, 146, 177, 66, 68-69, 98-99, 137, 141
Bearish Reversal Pattern, 273, 189, 191, 199, 112, 131
Bears, 273, 146-148, 162, 167, 169, 207, 52-54, 71, 82, 102, 115-117, 119, 122, 125, 127, 133-134
Bid Price, 273, 276
Blended Candle, 273, 176, 178, 5
Box Theory, 274, 198
Breakout, 274, 198, 222, 230, 240, 49, 109

Bull Market, 274, 195, 214, 45
Bullish Candle, 274, 177, 68, 119-120, 141
Bullish Reversal Pattern, 274, 185, 188, 138
Bulls, 264, 274, 150-152, 157, 166, 207, 237, 52, 55, 57, 63, 71, 97, 99, 107, 110-112, 120, 127, 132, 141

C

Call, 274, 21, 153, 41, 126
Candle Patterns, 265, 274, 21, 153, 195, 44, 65
CFD, 274
Commodities, 274, 15, 12
The Complete Guide to Using Candlestick Charting, 1-2, 9-10
Continuation Signal, 274, 150, 163

D

Dark Cloud Cover, 19, 146-147, 153, 181-182, 66-68, 81-82

Day Trader, 274, 276, 206

Derivative, 275, 192, 195

Descending Hawk, 73, 89

Diverge, 275

Doji, 267, 275, 19, 177-179, 181, 206, 237, 257, 36, 44-46, 48, 51-57, 62, 71-72, 81, 87-88, 94-96, 99-100, 114-115, 118, 143, 4

Downday, 275, 34

Downtrend, 274-275, 152, 157, 162-163, 168-171, 200, 222, 234, 239, 242, 247, 251, 50, 53-54, 62, 64, 70, 77, 83-84, 86, 88-91, 113-117, 119-123, 125, 127, 129, 133-136, 138

Dragonfly Doji, 53-55, 57

E

Engulf, 275

Equities, 275, 192, 254, 59, 79, 140

ETF, 275

Exit Point, 275

Exponential Moving Average, 263, 275, 185, 190

F

Fibonacci, 6, 184, 203-206, 210, 230, 275

Forex, 275-276, 12

Four-Price doji, 52

Fundamental Analysis:, 275, 280, 174, 40, 103-104

Futures, 276, 17, 225-226, 79, 12

G

Gravestone doji, 177, 237, 57, 62

H

Hammer, 264, 267, 20, 177, 54-55, 58, 61-62, 64, 81, 122, 143

Hanging Man, 267, 180, 55-56, 81, 143

High Wave Candle, 276, 47, 4

I

Index, 262, 273, 183, 189, 197, 256, 141-142, 2, 7

Indicator, 262-263, 273-274, 276-280, 155, 186-190, 196-197, 203, 227, 243, 256, 48, 53, 70, 72, 80, 95, 104, 109

Intraday, 276, 183, 193-194, 197, 30, 12

Inverted Hammer, 264, 62, 64, 143

L

Level II, 276, 228

Leverage, 276

Limit order, 276, 221-222

Line Chart, 276, 25

Liquidity, 276

Long-legged doji, 51-52

Lower Shadow, 277, 279, 34-37, 53-56, 63, 122, 136-137

M

MACD, 263-264, 277, 190-191, 256, 80, 104

Market order, 277, 220-221

Marubozu, 277, 36, 48, 69

Matching High, 74

Momentum, 277, 279, 183, 186, 193-194, 197, 234, 240, 66, 80, 88, 94, 100, 118-119

Moving Average, 263, 275, 277, 279, 183-185, 187, 190-191, 194, 201, 203, 206, 227, 252, 256, 60, 143

N

NASDAQ, 277, 18

Nison, Steve, 269, 18

NYSE, 273, 277, 18

O

OHLC, 277, 28-30

One Black Crow, 68-69, 84

Open Price, 30, 32

Option, 274-275, 277-278, 280, 225, 232

Oscillator, 263, 278, 280, 180, 186-189, 197, 256, 42, 144

Overbought, 262-263, 278, 183, 185, 188-189, 191, 197, 214, 235, 243, 27, 65, 139, 142, 144

Oversold, 262-263, 265, 267, 278, 180, 183, 185, 188-189, 191, 197, 206, 227, 243, 27, 63, 65, 105, 130, 133, 138, 142

P

Pivot Point, 278

Premium, 278

R

Relative Strength Indicator, 279

Resistance Line, 267, 278, 280, 48

Reversal Signal, 278, 149, 153, 178, 61, 65, 73, 75-76, 93, 121-122, 139

Risk/Reward, 279, 208, 228, 230, 14

S

Selling Short, 279, 222

Shadow, 268, 276-277, 279, 281, 229, 34-37, 45, 49, 53-56, 62-64, 76, 85, 96, 107, 112, 122, 127, 134-135, 137

Shares, 275, 277-281, 214, 220-222, 25-26, 57

Shaven Bottom, 279, 35, 63

Shaven Head, 279, 35, 56

Shooting Star, 177, 237, 58, 61-62, 81, 143

Short-Term Trader, 269, 279, 22

Signal Line, 263-264, 267, 279,

187, 190-191

Simple Moving Average, 279, 184, 201, 252, 143

Spinning Top, 265, 279, 181, 237, 46-47, 81, 4

Spread, 280, 196, 202

Star, 280, 167, 177, 181, 236-237, 58, 61-62, 72, 81, 88, 93-97, 99-100, 111, 113-115, 118, 126, 143

Stochastic Oscillator, 280, 180, 186-189, 256

Stop-Loss, 280, 197, 199, 210, 221, 223-225, 228-230

Stopping Out, 280

Strike price, 280

Support And Resistance, 268, 280, 21, 183, 197-199, 201, 230, 38, 48, 76, 14, 6

Support Line, 280, 185, 48

Swing Trading, 280, 79, 140

T

Technical Analysis, 280, 17, 20, 22, 174, 183, 186, 202, 236, 26-27, 38, 40-41, 79, 104, 141, 143, 9-10

Trading Plan, 264, 273, 281, 209-210, 212-213, 216-217, 226-227, 229, 254, 41-42, 80, 6

Trailing Stop, 281, 222, 238

Trigger, 264, 281, 185, 188-189, 191, 194, 207, 243, 30, 59-61

Tweezer Top, 268, 76, 91

U

Upday, 281, 34

Upper Shadow, 268, 276, 279, 281, 34-37, 54-55, 62-63, 76, 107, 112, 134-135

Uptrend, 262-263, 281, 146, 148, 150, 155-159, 165-168, 171, 177, 182, 185, 200, 202, 204, 206, 234, 237, 239, 241-242, 246-247, 250-251, 254, 45, 53, 55, 57, 61-62, 66-70, 72-75, 94-98, 101, 103, 106-108, 110-112, 131

V

Volatility, 281, 183, 195, 201-203, 230, 60, 6

Volume, 265-268, 281, 18, 21, 148, 180, 183, 194, 207, 239, 253, 255, 257-259, 26, 42, 45-46, 50, 52, 60, 66, 71, 73, 77, 80, 86, 99, 101-102, 104-105, 118-120, 135-136, 142

W

White Real Body, 34, 66, 94